Edited by Naomi Starkey September–December 2007

Suggestions for using *New Daylight*

Find a regular time and place, if possible, where you can read and pray undisturbed. Before you begin, take time to be still and perhaps use the BRF prayer. Then read the Bible passage slowly (try reading it aloud if you find it over-familiar), followed by the comment. You can also use *New Daylight* for group study and discussion, if you prefer.

The prayer or point for reflection can be a starting point for your own meditation and prayer. Many people like to keep a journal to record their thoughts about a Bible passage and items for prayer. In *New Daylight* we also note the Sundays and special festivals from the Church calendar, to keep in step with the Christian year.

New Daylight and the Bible

New Daylight contributors use a range of Bible versions, and you will find a list of the versions used in each issue at the back of the notes on page 154. You are welcome to use your own preferred version alongside the passage printed in the notes, and this can be particularly helpful if the Bible text has been abridged.

New Daylight affirms that the whole of the Bible is God's revelation to us, and we should read, reflect on and learn from every part of both Old and New Testaments. Usually the printed comment presents a straight-forward 'thought for the day', but sometimes it may also raise questions rather than simply providing answers, as we wrestle with some of the more difficult passages of Scripture.

Writers in this issue

Jennifer Oldroyd worked for many years at the Ashburnham Place conference centre in East Sussex. She was Managing Editor for a major Christian publisher and, in the last few years, has had published two books of study material for small groups.

Margaret Silf is an ecumenical Christian, committed to working across and beyond the denominational divides. For most of her working life she was employed in the computer industry, but left paid employment to devote herself to writing and accompanying others on their spiritual journey.

Stephen Rand works for Open Doors, a charity supporting the persecuted church, while also being co-chair of Jubilee Debt Campaign and part of the leadership team of a Baptist church in Wimbledon that meets to worship in the local Odeon cinema. Stephen is the author of BRF's book of Advent readings, *When the Time Was Right* (2006).

Helen Julian CSF is an Anglican Franciscan sister, currently serving her community as Minister Provincial. She has written *Living the Gospel*, *The Lindisfarne Icon* and *The Road to Emmaus* for BRF.

Rachel Boulding is Deputy Editor of the *Church Times*. For some years she was Senior Editor at SPCK Publishing, commissioning religious books. She lives with her husband and young son in Dorset.

Veronica Zundel is an Oxford graduate, writer and journalist. She lives with her husband and young son in North London, where they belong to the Mennonite Church.

David Winter is retired from parish ministry. An honorary Canon of Christ Church, Oxford, he is well known as a writer and broadcaster. He is a Series Editor of *The People's Bible Comentary*.

John Proctor is married to Elaine, with two adult children. He works for the United Reformed Church, teaching the New Testament to students in Cambridge. Before that he was a parish minister in Glasgow. John has written *The People's Bible Commentary: Matthew* (BRF, 2001) and *Urban God* (BRF, 2002).

David Robertson has ministered in a variety of parishes since his ordination in 1979 and is currently a vicar in Halifax. He has written *Marriage—Restoring Our Vision* and *Collaborative Ministry* for BRF.

Further BRF reading for this issue

For more in-depth coverage of some of the passages in these Bible reading notes, we recommend the following titles:

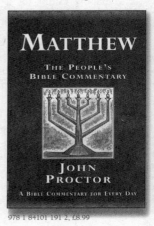

978 1 84101 191 2, £8.99

978 1 84101 066 3, £8.99

978 1 84101 094 6, £7.99

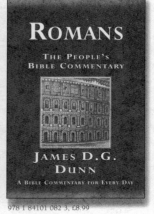

978 1 84101 082 3, £8.99

Naomi Starkey writes...

I may have said this before—but commissioning *New Daylight* sometimes feels like doing a large and complicated jigsaw. As it happens, I like doing jigsaws (probably a good thing, under the circumstances) but it can still be a challenge to fit all the pieces into a coherent whole.

I start a year before the first deadline, and two years before publication, with a blank calendar template for three issues at a time. Checking through my database of contents for previous issues, I decide which books of the Bible are due for coverage. Obviously some lend themselves more readily to daily readings than others—and that's where the themes, overviews and character studies come in.

The jigsaw aspect comes to the fore when I begin considering the possible subjects against the Church calendar. *New Daylight* always has specific weeks of readings for Easter and Christmas, but we also regularly include material relating to other special festivals. It can be helpful, too, to have occasional sets of readings linking to the seasonal activities of daily life—going on holiday, start of the new school year, New Year's resolutions, and so on.

Finally, I work my way through the contributor team, trying to match writers up with their interests and strengths, and whether they have requested to cover a particular section of the Bible. When the plans are complete, I discuss them with colleagues in case they spot any potential problems (too much gloomy Old Testament in November or February, for example).

When it all comes together, it is very satisfying; but sometimes the best-shaped plans prove flawed, for a whole variety of reasons... I am pleased to say, though, that *New Daylight* readers are, on the whole, a fairly understanding and forgiving bunch when this happens!

So what are some of the highlights for September to December 2007? Well, we have Veronica Zundel completing the book of Job, and Helen Julian on 'Stewards of creation', readings connecting with Animal Welfare Sunday (7 October).

We have David Winter writing three weeks on Romans 1—8 (partly in response to readers requesting more verse-by-verse readings); the rest of Romans will be covered in autumn 2008. And we also have two short sets of readings by Margaret Silf, first 'Words of hope' and then 'Words of peace', which I hope will prove helpful in the hectic pre-Christmas days.

The BRF Prayer

Almighty God,
you have taught us that your word is a lamp for our feet
and a light for our path. Help us, and all who prayerfully
read your word, to deepen our fellowship with each other
through your love. And in so doing may we come to know you
more fully, love you more truly, and follow more faithfully in
the steps of your son Jesus Christ, who lives and reigns with
you and the Holy Spirit, one God for evermore. Amen.

2 Timothy

'Why is it that other people seem so strong, so confident, so prayerful, so devoted to Bible study, so brave in witnessing?' If you sometimes say that—or something similar—to yourself, can you imagine what the Christian life must have been like for Timothy? The great apostle Paul was his mentor, his hero, his father in God. He had accompanied Paul on his missionary journeys, he had been prayed for by Paul, and he had been commissioned by him to care for the church in Ephesus. But he must have been always conscious of his own weakness and his own lack of confidence.

Paul's first letter to Timothy had given detailed instructions about the ordering of church life. Now, two years later, Paul is once again in prison. This time he is not simply under house arrest as before (Acts 28:16). Now it is rather more serious, and he is facing execution. It may be that he is actually in a cell or dungeon. He is cold ('bring my cloak', see 2 Timothy 4:13) and he wonders if he will survive the winter (v. 21). From here he composes the last letter he will write. It is to his dearly beloved Timothy.

Bearing in mind the relationship between these two men, the letter often seems touchingly personal and private. Love and longing shine through. But there are also indications that Paul shares Timothy's doubts about the younger man's abilities. Timothy is so young, so untried, so lacking in the powerful personality that God used to such effect in Paul's own ministry. How is he going to manage a church filled with overly clever scholars and time wasters? How is he going to fight the fight, finish the race, keep the faith (4:7)? In answer to his own doubts and anxieties, Paul writes this letter. It is like a hand stretched out from the older man to the younger. It tries, through instruction and exhortation, to grasp Timothy's hand and pull him into a safer, more mature place in the kingdom.

If you feel unworthy for the position you hold or if you have doubts about your own 'commission', then this is the epistle for you. Read it and take hold of the tools that Paul writes about—tools that, through the Holy Spirit, will help to make you 'strong in the grace that is in Christ Jesus' (2:1).

Jennifer Oldroyd

Rekindle the gift

Paul, an apostle of Christ Jesus by the will of God, for the sake of the promise of life that is in Christ Jesus, to Timothy, my beloved child: Grace, mercy, and peace from God the Father and Christ Jesus our Lord. I am grateful to God—whom I worship with a clear conscience, as my ancestors did—when I remember you constantly in my prayers night and day. Recalling your tears, I long to see you so that I may be filled with joy. I am reminded of your sincere faith, a faith that lived first in your grandmother Lois and your mother Eunice and now, I am sure, lives in you. For this reason I remind you to rekindle the gift of God that is within you through the laying on of my hands; for God did not give us a spirit of cowardice, but rather a spirit of power and of love and of self-discipline.

As Paul begins this letter, he hands Timothy the first key to 'the promise of life' (v. 1): Timothy is to look to the past. Paul knew the power in having ancestors who have loved God (v. 3). Timothy could not claim the impeccable lineage of Paul (see Romans 11:1), but he had a believing grandmother and a believing mother. He had an inheritance. Never underestimate the influence of the faith of those who have gone before, and never stop praying for the generations to come.

Second, Paul reminds Timothy of his commissioning. I am always deeply moved by ordination services, in whichever tradition they take place. The word 'sacrament' is often applied to these occasions. In the words of Cranmer's Book of Common Prayer, a sacrament is 'an outward and visible sign of an inward and spiritual grace'. When Timothy was ordained and Paul laid his hands upon him (v. 6), something happened in the spiritual realm: God the Holy Spirit conferred upon him power, love and self-discipline (v. 7)—the very things he needed!

Look to your past today. Remember those who have prayed for you. Remember those times when you have been ordained, commissioned or simply prayed for, and rekindle the gift of God that was given to you on those occasions.

Prayer

Almighty God, help me to remember the people and the things that have made me what I am, and help me to be that person today. Amen

JO

Do not be ashamed

Do not be ashamed, then, of the testimony about our Lord or of me his prisoner, but join with me in suffering for the gospel, relying on the power of God, who saved us and called us with a holy calling... For this gospel I was appointed a herald and an apostle and a teacher, and for this reason I suffer as I do. But I am not ashamed, for I know the one in whom I have put my trust, and I am sure that he is able to guard until that day what I have entrusted to him... Onesiphorus... often refreshed me and was not ashamed of my chain.

I have picked out of today's passage the three references to being ashamed. I imagine it must have been very hard to be a friend and associate of Paul—even when he was in full flow as a preacher and apostle, let alone when he was in prison. But Paul urges Timothy not only to stand by him and to be unashamed of his association with a condemned man but also actually to join with him in suffering for the gospel (v. 8).

Ephesus was an important centre for commerce, politics and religion. Those who listened to Timothy's preaching would not have been simple people, happy with a simple faith in Jesus of Nazareth. They would have been sophisticated intellectuals, endlessly prepared to discuss theological niceties and speculations, and perhaps inclined to be dismissive of Timothy's gospel message.

Often it's not persecution that we have to bear—it's embarrassment. We see the surprise, the disbelieving laughter, the sneer, because we claim to believe in God and to have a relationship with him. And there is often no admiration for a lifestyle based on Christian values. If you remain a virgin until you marry or if you have elderly relatives to live with you or if you adopt a simple lifestyle, you may be mocked for your naivety. 'The world is just not like that any more,' some will say.

Don't be ashamed of your calling today. Join with all those who suffer for the gospel around the world, and rely on the power of the God who has saved and called you.

Prayer

Forgive me, Lord, for the times when I have been ashamed of you and your calling. Help me to trust you today for courage to do what you have called me to do. Amen

JO

Be strong

*You then, my child, be strong in the grace that is in Christ Jesus...
No one serving in the army gets entangled in everyday affairs; the
soldier's aim is to please the enlisting officer. And in the case of an
athlete, no one is crowned without competing according to the
rules. It is the farmer who does the work who ought to have the first
share of the crops. Think over what I say, for the Lord will give you
understanding in all things... The saying is sure: If we have died
with him, we will also live with him; if we endure, we will also reign
with him; if we deny him, he will also deny us; if we are faithless,
he remains faithful—for he cannot deny himself.*

Even a superficial reading of the
Acts of the Apostles and some of
the epistles will show us that Paul
was an incredibly hard worker. He
travelled widely, he taught untir-
ingly, he argued and reasoned and
prayed—and then set about making tents to raise the money for the
next trip.

Timothy, on the other hand,
does not leave quite the same
impression on us, and we may
wonder how he felt at receiving
these three word pictures from
Paul, urging him to fight like a soldier, train like an athlete and work
like a farmer.

But Paul is right, and the prin-
ciples remain just as true today. As
the computer experts say, 'Garbage
in—garbage out!' How much effort
are you putting into the commission that God has given you? Are
you as disciplined as a soldier? Are
you as firm with your body and

mind as an athlete? Are you as
hardworking as a farmer?

Many of us live in a culture
where life is relatively easy, and
where we are being persuaded
every day to give ourselves a treat
'because you're worth it'. We need
to do as Paul suggests and think
about these three illustrations. He
promises that the Lord will give
understanding—and that promise,
praise God, is as true today as it
was when Paul first wrote it.

Prayer

*Lord Jesus, have I gone soft and
flabby as a Christian? Please show
me today where I need to be more
disciplined, more committed and
more hard-working. Amen.*

JO

The word of truth

Remind them of this, and warn them before God that they are to avoid wrangling over words, which does not good but only ruins those who are listening. Do your best to present yourself to God as one approved by him, a worker who has no need to be ashamed, rightly explaining the word of truth. Avoid profane chatter, for it will lead people into more and more impiety, and their talk will spread like gangrene... But God's firm foundation stands, bearing this inscription: 'The Lord know those who are his', and, 'Let everyone who calls on the name of the Lord turn away from wickedness.'

Paul's warning to Timothy of the dangers of chatter, fruitless argument and 'wrangling over words' (v. 14) was also given in his first letter (see 1 Timothy 1:4). Timothy was never going to be able to bludgeon people into the kingdom with words. Instead, he had to apprentice himself to Jesus, the living Word, and learn how to use words to 'rightly explain the word of truth' (see v. 15).

Paul had a lot of experience of preaching and teaching. He had ministered in many places and knew how people often love to discuss 'religion' generally. They are not seeking peace with God or the salvation of their souls, but simply want to spend an hour or two in stimulating conversation. Maybe the fact that Paul addresses the issue again in this second letter is an indication of the situation in Ephesus, and of Timothy's problems with time wasters.

The answer, says Paul, is to understand that 'the Lord knows those who are his' (v. 19). If we stay close to God and listen carefully to him, then we will spend our time, our effort and our prayer on the people he is already drawing to himself, and our words will help them towards the kingdom. This surely is what Jesus did: 'The Son can do nothing on his own, but only what he sees the Father doing' (John 5:19).

Meditation

'A word fitly spoken is like apples of gold in a setting of silver. Like a gold ring or an ornament of gold is a wise rebuke to a listening ear. Like the cold of snow in the time of harvest are faithful messengers to those who send them; they refresh the spirit of their masters'
(Proverbs 25:11–13).

JO

Dedicated and useful

In a large house there are utensils not only of gold and silver but also of wood and clay, some for special use, some for ordinary. All who cleanse themselves of the things I have mentioned will become special utensils, dedicated and useful to the owner of the house, ready for every good work. Shun youthful passions and pursue righteousness, faith, love, and peace, along with those who call on the Lord from a pure heart... And the Lord's servant must not be quarrelsome but kindly to everyone, an apt teacher, patient, correcting opponents with gentleness. God may perhaps grant that they will repent and come to know the truth, and that they may escape from the snare of the devil, having been held captive by him to do his will.

Reading these verses, we may wonder whether, at some point, Timothy had stumbled. Had he lost his temper with some argumentative church member? Had he become too close to someone of the opposite sex in his desire to convince and convert? There is nothing harsh in Paul's words. Indeed, he seems to be making an effort to be gentle and encouraging. But still these verses sound like a rebuke. 'What sort of vessel do you want to be...? Cleanse yourself... shun youthful passions... don't be quarrelsome... correct people with gentleness.'

Have you got someone who is prepared to talk to you about your weaknesses? I recently attended the thanksgiving service for a great evangelical writer, speaker and counsellor. One of the most telling testimonies to his ministry was from a counselling colleague who shared the fact that this man had dared to challenge him over certain things in his teaching.

If you want to be a gold plate in the house of God rather than a wooden spoon, then you need all the help you can get. Advice, criticism and rebuke can all help you to cleanse yourself and to become dedicated and useful. It works the other way round, too. We should be prepared to challenge others when we see something wrong in their life—not to condemn but to help them 'escape from the snare of the devil' (v. 26).

Prayer

Almighty God, send me friends prepared to be critics, and critics prepared to be friends. Amen

JO

Avoid them!

You must understand this, that in the last days distressing times will come. For people will be lovers of themselves, lovers of money, boasters, arrogant, abusive, disobedient to their parents, ungrateful, unholy, inhuman, implacable, slanderers, profligates, brutes, haters of good, treacherous, reckless, swollen with conceit, lovers of pleasure rather than lovers of God, holding to the outward form of godliness but denying its power. Avoid them! ... But they will not make much progress, because... their folly will become plain to everyone.

Who is Paul describing here? At the end of his list of undesirables, he writes of those who are 'holding to the outward form of godliness but denying its power' (v. 5). Paul is talking about church members, and introducing Timothy to a fact of life that ought to be borne in mind by every minister, youth leader, Sunday school teacher and group leader: there are people who have an outward form of godliness but no inner life with God.

Let's look at some of the words Paul uses. First, 'abusive': there are those who call it 'teasing' but who are always putting other people down or belittling their partners in public. Or 'implacable': there are people who always criticize and never say anything positive about the church and its ministry. Or 'treacherous': there are people who gossip about others and often give away confidences. Go through the list and think how these things might manifest themselves in our churches and fellowships today.

The answer (and this from a great evangelist, pastor and teacher!) is to avoid such people. Paul suggests that there may come times in the life of a church or fellowship when it is right to set aside the opinions of those who would block the work of God, to avoid them and to move ahead without them: they won't make progress and they will hold the rest back.

What a dangerous idea to introduce to a young, inexperienced pastor! But such situations are, says Paul, indicative of 'the last days' (v. 1) and, distressing though they may be, Timothy is not to shrink from them.

Meditation

'Do not give what is holy to dogs; and do not throw your pearls before swine, or they will trample them under foot and turn and maul you' (Matthew 7:6).

JO

13

I solemnly urge you...

Now you have observed my teaching, my conduct, my aim in life, my faith, my patience, my love, my steadfastness, my persecutions, and my suffering... But as for you, continue in what you have learned and firmly believed, knowing from whom you learned it, and how from childhood you have known the sacred writings that are able to instruct you for salvation through faith in Christ Jesus. All scripture is inspired by God and is useful for teaching, for reproof, for correction, and for training in righteousness... I solemnly urge you: proclaim the message; be persistent whether the time is favourable or unfavourable; convince, rebuke, and encourage, with the utmost patience in teaching.

Paul now reaches the climax of his letter. The passage is shortened here, but do read it all through if you can, imagining Paul's hopes and fears and sensing his urgency. How is he going to help this young man to succeed?

First, he tells Timothy never to forget his example. Paul will be gone soon, but he has left a legacy of love, patience, teaching and conduct that Timothy can remember and feed on for the future. Are you living in such a way that you could say to a new Christian, 'Watch what I do. This is how to be a Christian'?

Second, Paul points back to scripture: everything we need is there. Read the Bible. Read great chunks of it. Read it at night until you fall asleep. Read it in the bath. Read it on the train.

Finally, Paul lays a solemn charge on Timothy. He doesn't put him on the rota for preaching or leading worship. He recognizes God's calling and, 'in the presence of God and of Christ Jesus, who is to judge the living and the dead, and in view of his appearing and his kingdom' (4:1), he commissions him—to proclaim the message, to suffer, to work and to carry out the ministry to which he has been called.

Have you been commissioned to do any kind of task in the church of God? If so, these words to Timothy can be for you too. Listen to Paul, learn from him and rededicate yourself to serving Timothy's God and yours.

Prayer
Thank you, Father, for your calling. Fill me with your Spirit today, so that I can be what you want me to be.

JO

To him be the glory for ever

As for me, I am already being poured out as a libation, and the time of my departure has come. I have fought the good fight, I have finished the race, I have kept the faith. From now on there is reserved for me the crown of righteousness, which the Lord, the righteous judge, will give to me on that day... Do your best to come to me soon... Get Mark and bring him with you... When you come, bring the cloak that I left with Carpus at Troas, also the books, and above all the parchments... The Lord will rescue me from every evil attack and save me for his heavenly kingdom. To him be the glory for ever and ever. Amen... The Lord be with your spirit. Grace be with you.

After the heights of yesterday, today's passage feels like missing the last stair: we come down to earth with a bump. Once again, we have shortened the reading, but look at the whole passage, and at the very human face that Paul shows in his final words.

He feels death approaching, but he is looking forward to his reward. He is remembering the hard times, those who opposed him and those who deserted him. He is remembering the good friends he made in his years of ministry and sending them his greetings. And he is longing to see Timothy one more time.

As we read the Bible, it is all too easy to think that the characters portrayed are like the heroes invented for children's stories or like the superheroes in comic books and films. Verses like these help us to see very clearly that the people who appear in the pages of the word of God were men and women, just like us. They shared our weaknesses and our doubts. They shared our sins and our failings—and when we read of their battles, their victories and their failures, we can identify with them and learn from them.

Pray today that when you come to the last chapter of your life, you will be able to face death as Paul did, in the consciousness that you have fought the fight, finished the race and kept the faith.

Prayer

Almighty God, be glorified in my life today, and when my race is run, be glorified in my death. Amen

JO

One step at a time

The Lord exists for ever; your word is firmly fixed in heaven. Your faithfulness endures to all generations; you have established the earth, and it stands fast. By your appointment they stand today, for all things are your servants. If your law had not been my delight, I would have perished in my misery. I will not forget your precepts, for by them you have given me life... Your word is a lamp to my feet and a light to my path.

There are not many places left where we experience anything like complete darkness, but one such place lingers in my memory. It was just a small village in the Cumbrian hills, dark enough on a moonless winter night for the unwary walker to go seriously astray. Sometimes, during holidays there, I would go for a nocturnal walk, carrying a small pocket torch. The pool of light it shed was just about sufficient to illuminate the ground immediately in front of my feet. If I tried to focus the beam on to the road ahead, the light would simply be swallowed up by the ravenous night. I quickly learned to be content with seeing just one step ahead.

The words of hope today might have been written for someone stumbling along in the dark like that. 'However shaky I may be feeling, the Lord is firm. If it were not so, I would have lost my way long ago.' God is like that beam of light, unfailingly lighting up our next step, while we keep straining to see a few miles ahead so that we can make plans and take control.

Control isn't on offer. Instead, we are asked to trust—to focus our gaze on the pool of God's light in the present moment and not on the darkness that still lies ahead. Our hope is in the promise that amid all the confusion and obscurity of our life's pathway, the next step will be illuminated by God's love and grace. It's a promise we can trust. God has been faithful all along the journey so far, and he will not fail us in the steps that lie ahead, provided we take them one at a time.

Reflection

Try living today one moment at a time, paying attention to God's light shining on your next step.

MS

Winter into spring

For as the rain and the snow come down from heaven, and do not return there until they have watered the earth, making it bring forth and sprout, giving seed to the sower and bread to the eater, so shall my word be that goes out from my mouth; it shall not return to me empty, but it shall accomplish that which I purpose, and succeed in the thing for which I sent it. For you shall go out in joy, and be led back in peace; the mountains and the hills before you shall burst into song, and all the trees of the field shall clap their hands.

One memorable springtime, as I recall, creation leapt to life in just a single week. One week the world was still grey and cold; the next it was throbbing with birdsong and yellow with daffodils.

It didn't happen by magic. It happened because all through the winter months the frost and snow had broken up the earth and the rain had soaked into the cracks and furrows. The weather that seemed so chilling and forbidding to us as we gazed disconsolately out of our streaming windows was actually nurturing all this springtime glory—two faces of the same loving, life-giving Creator in whom every drop of rain, every gust of wind and every piercing frost has a purpose.

The prophet tells us that the winter storms and downpours come from the skies and do not return until they have fulfilled their purpose. What is true of the rains and the snows that fall upon the wintering earth is surely also true of the hard experiences in our own lives—the times when we too feel cold and alone, abandoned, swamped or suffocated by adversity. Can these things also be part of God's great purpose, the purpose of growth and life?

We grow most readily when we are least comfortable. The seeds of our true nature are often nourished and brought to life by things we wish would not have happened. Our hope is in God's promise that he, and we too, shall one day shout out in joy over all that has grown in the fields of our hearts.

Reflection

Can you, in hindsight, see any times when 'winter weather' in your own life has nurtured new life?

MS

After the locusts

I will repay you for the years that the swarming locust has eaten... And my people shall never again be put to shame. You shall know that I am in the midst of Israel, and that I, the Lord, am your God and there is no other. And my people shall never again be put to shame. Then afterwards I will pour out my spirit on all flesh; your sons and daughters shall prophesy, your old men shall dream dreams, and your young men shall see visions. Even on the male and female slaves, in those days, I will pour out my spirit.

In her book *Away* (Bloomsbury, 2002), Jane Urquhart tells the poignant story of an Irish family, forced to emigrate to North America during the famine. They had been promised a patch of land to farm on their arrival. The parents didn't survive the voyage, but the two adolescent children were given their land and tried to farm it. Their labours were literally fruitless. The land was on the hard rock of the Canadian Shield. Farming it was a thankless, futile task.

Eventually, in desperation, the two children, now grown, moved on. Soon after their departure, seams of gold were found beneath the intractable surface of the land.

This story took my thoughts back to fruitless areas of my own life—perhaps tasks I never could accomplish or relationships I never could make work, however hard I tried. These are like the 'years that the swarming locust has eaten' and sometimes I want to weep for their loss. Yet the story of the Irish migrants reminds me that I have sometimes found seams of gold beneath the surface of these apparently devastating failures. Perhaps I have learned something important about myself or discovered a deeper empathy with those who suffer. In hindsight, I can see how God has indeed blessed me with more than I could ever have known if there hadn't been any locusts.

Today's word of hope is that God's Spirit is always more powerful than any number of locusts, and it will turn our finest dreams and visions into living reality.

Reflection

Some parts of our life experience are not meant to be farmed, but mined. What seams of gold have you discovered beneath your life's failed crops?

MS

The creation of a masterpiece

For surely I know the plans I have for you, says the Lord, plans for your welfare and not for harm, to give you a future with hope. Then when you call upon me and come and pray to me, I will hear you. When you search for me, you will find me; if you seek me with all your heart, I will let you find me, says the Lord, and I will restore your fortunes and gather you from all the nations and all the places where I have driven you, says the Lord, and I will bring you back to the place from which I sent you into exile.

Sometimes I wonder what a fly might see if it crawled across the surface of the Sistine Chapel ceiling. I imagine it having a quiet conversation with itself: 'Oh, today the world is so dark. I can't see any point in it. Why does my life have to be so black? What's the purpose of it all?'

Of course, the next day, when it has crawled a bit further, the day might dawn bright with gold and crimson and life would take on a very different hue for the roaming fly. What it would never know, however, was that it was actually navigating a masterpiece.

Although in God's eyes we are, of course, worth infinitely more than our fly on the wall, God might still hear our complaints as we plod across the picture of our lives, and long to touch our hearts with his reassurance: 'Trust me. You are navigating a work of art. You can't yet see its grandeur and beauty, but I am the artist who is creating the masterpiece that is your life and I know the plans I have for it. Can you trust me for its unfolding?'

Today's word of hope assures us that there is meaning in what we see as chaos, and a purpose where we see only futility. There is a homecoming too—to the place in God's heart where one day we shall see the masterpiece and come into the eternal presence of the one who brings it to fulfilment.

Reflection

Your life is a masterpiece of God's creativity. If you seek him in it, you will find him there.

MS

Thinking big with little things

[Jesus] put before them another parable: 'The kingdom of heaven is like a mustard seed that someone took and sowed in his field; it is the smallest of all the seeds, but when it has grown it is the greatest of shrubs and becomes a tree, so that the birds of the air come and make nests in its branches.' He told them another parable: 'The kingdom of heaven is like yeast that a woman took and mixed in with three measures of flour until all of it was leavened.' Jesus told the crowds all these things in parables; without a parable he told them nothing.

Jesus had a special fondness for little things. He used many parables to explain how the kingdom of heaven is a miracle of tiny beginnings—a little seed, a small measure of yeast, a little child. This is amazingly good news, because 'small' is what most of us do best! We are good at making a small effort here and there or putting in a little word or making an apparently insignificant gesture. Today's word of hope tells us, unequivocally, that huge things grow from these small beginnings.

Maybe you have sometimes wondered if your own little life can seriously make any difference to the coming of God's reign on planet earth? If so, just think back, in your imagination, to the moment you were conceived. How big were you then? But what enormous potential lay furled up in that single cell, too small to view with the naked eye—and how wonderfully that potential has unfurled and revealed itself in the passing years of your life so far. Or think back to the moment maybe 15 billion years ago (so scientists currently reckon) when our whole universe was just a 'singularity', an infinitesimally tiny entity, but containing, in potential, a cosmos far too vast for us to measure or comprehend.

Yes, God thinks big with tiny things.

If God can grow a unique 'you' from a single cell and a whole universe from an entity smaller than a grain of salt, we can indeed hope and trust that he can grow a kingdom from a simple act of kindness.

Reflection

Seeds of love grow into trees of hope and forests of faith.

MS

I know my own

[Jesus said] 'I am the good shepherd. The good shepherd lays down his life for the sheep. The hired hand, who is not the shepherd and does not own the sheep, sees the wolf coming and leaves the sheep and runs away—and the wolf snatches them and scatters them. The hired hand runs away because a hired hand does not care for the sheep. I am the good shepherd. I know my own and my own know me, just as the Father knows me and I know the Father. And I lay down my life for the sheep. I have other sheep that do not belong to this fold. I must bring them also, and they will listen to my voice. So there will be one flock, one shepherd.'

There are many intangible connections that link parent to child. One of them is voice. The voice of a loved child calling for you will instantly break through everything else and send you in search of them. It works across a crowded supermarket and it even works at two in the morning through the heaviest of sleep. You know your own child and your own child knows you.

It also works in the animal kingdom. Imagine a barn full of bats. Thousands of baby bats are hanging from the rafters, squealing for a meal, while the parent bats go out in search of food. It's the dead of night. The barn is pitch black. The parents return with supper. So how do they find their own baby bat? Answer: each bat squeals on a unique frequency. Parents and offspring immediately know their own and their own know them.

Isn't it a bit like that with prayer? When we try to pray, the words may get in the way, but our desire for prayer alone is sufficient to connect us to the heart of God in a unique way.

Our word of hope today is that nothing can ever disconnect us from the God who loves us and listens out for us continuously, whether we are tuned in or not.

Reflection

God recognizes the voice of our longing before ever we can put it into words, and he responds with the love of the one who gives his life for us.

MS

God hasn't finished yet

Love never ends. But as for prophecies, they will come to an end; as for tongues, they will cease; as for knowledge, it will come to an end. For we know only in part, and we prophesy only in part; but when the complete comes, the partial will come to an end. When I was a child, I spoke like a child, I thought like a child, I reasoned like a child; when I became an adult, I put an end to childish ways. For now we see in a mirror, dimly, but then we will see face to face. Now I know only in part; then I will know fully, even as I have been fully known. And now faith, hope, and love abide, these three; and the greatest of these is love.

After a minor falling-out with my small daughter one day, she disarmed me completely with a little prayer card. It showed a kitten standing in a pool of milk beside an upturned saucer and looking very woebegone. The caption read, 'Please be patient. God hasn't finished with me yet!' Needless to say, my anger melted and I still cherish that card, nearly 20 years after the event.

God hasn't finished with any of us yet—and that is today's word of hope. Whatever kind of mess we feel ourselves to be in, however many unfinished projects and broken dreams lie around us, God hasn't finished with us. Paul reminds us that all we can see is the first draft of the great work we shall become, the messy underpainting of the masterpiece that God is dreaming into being.

This applies to matters both small and great. We tend to think that we are always at the leading edge of human knowledge, but the latest insights of science and technology will move on tomorrow, for sure. In the same way, we ourselves are constantly 'work in progress', in the hands of the one who made us and nurtures all our growth.

There is a further word of hope: 'Love never ends'. God hasn't finished with us yet, but God is holding us constantly in an embrace of love that will not fail, however incomplete we are and however dim our present vision.

Reflection

To lose our illusions is to come a step closer to the truth. The pain of disillusionment may be the beginning of a whole new season of growth.

MS

Exodus 8—14:
Freedom and deliverance

Here is a defining story of the Bible. It shaped a whole nation's understanding of God and it has inspired generations upon generations, right up to the present time, to believe that, however dark the situation may be, God will deliver his people.

It's an appropriate narrative to read in the year in which we are celebrating the bicentenary of the ending of the transatlantic slave trade. The story of Exodus is a story in which the oppressor is forced to concede his power and the slaves are set free; it's a story of God at work in human history, doing justice in the context of mercy.

Tradition suggests that the story is written by Moses, the man at the heart of the events described. He would certainly have known more than most about what took place—but Moses was a prophet and this is history written by a prophet. That does not mean that the history is unreliable or the facts distorted. It does mean, though, that it is history written to help people understand the ways of God.

So here you will find great themes of redemption, salvation, justice and mercy introduced and explained in the language of story. The themes and symbols will be developed and explored elsewhere in scripture and find fulfilment in another story—that of God loving the world so much that he gave his one and only Son, so that whoever believes in him shall not perish but have eternal life (John 3:16).

The story of Exodus is ultimately one of a spiritual battle. Pharaoh is a human king who believes himself to have the power of a god and therefore the right to absolute authority and obedience. But only the one true God has that right, and whenever that right is contested, whether by human or spiritual forces, then battle is joined —the battle between good and evil.

We begin our readings with battle already underway. Pharaoh has enslaved the people of God and abused his power to the extent that he has ordered every baby boy to be killed at birth. He has turned the screw of forced labour so hard that the people are at breaking point, crying out to God in their distress. God hears them and God acts.

Stephen Rand

Let my people go

Then the Lord said to Moses, 'Go to Pharaoh and say to him, "This is what the Lord says: let my people go, so that they may worship me. If you refuse to let them go, I will send a plague of frogs on your whole country. The Nile will teem with frogs. They will come up into your palace and your bedroom and onto your bed, into the houses of your officials and on your people, and into your ovens and kneading troughs. The frogs will come up on you and your people and all your officials."'

I suspect that the last thing you need, right now, is to be thinking about frogs in your bed! Welcome to the disgusting reality of the battle for total authority between the god-king Pharaoh of Egypt and Almighty God, King of kings.

This was a significant and massive spiritual battle; it inevitably had awful material and physical outcomes. With today's materialistic outlook, the reality of the spiritual is often ignored or regarded as a separate compartment of life that can be investigated by those who are interested. Even Christians are not all convinced that spiritual warfare is a reality.

Yet all around us we see the human cost of rebellion against God: brokenness, despair and heartache revealed in drug taking, child abuse and violence. How much we need the evil one to be forced to 'let my people go'! You will recall that the first plague had been the Nile turning to blood. As we shall see, it was to take blood of a different kind to break the chains of evil—in Egypt, then at Calvary.

Perhaps it was the pollution of the Nile that forced the frogs from their natural habitat. Much scientific thought has been given to the succession of natural disasters that befell the Egyptian land and people, but Pharaoh knew that they were natural disasters with supernatural dimensions and timing that revealed a spiritual reality.

The Hebrew words translated 'plague' mean both a 'blow' and a 'sign'. Pharaoh was discovering that the God he had abused by enslaving his people and refusing to repent was a God who would not allow sin to go unpunished (the 'blow' of judgment) but would also 'signpost' his offer of mercy.

Prayer
Lord God, help us to understand the signs of the times. Amen

SR

The battle intensifies

Then the Lord said to Moses, 'Get up early in the morning, confront Pharaoh and say to him, "… By now I could have stretched out my hand and struck you and your people with a plague that would have wiped you off the earth. But I have raised you up for this very purpose, that I might show you my power and that my name might be proclaimed in all the earth. You still set yourself against my people and will not let them go. Therefore, at this time tomorrow I will send the worst hailstorm that has ever fallen on Egypt…"' Those officials of Pharaoh who feared the word of the Lord hurried to bring their slaves and their livestock inside.

The war is intensifying as blow after blow falls on the stronghold of opposition to God. The frogs died in their millions, and it is possible that the consequent stinking putrefaction released the next plague, an infestation of 'gnats'. Then myriad flying insects filled the homes of the Egyptians and, as Pharaoh remained unmoved, what had been appallingly unpleasant became economically threatening: the livestock were struck down. This was followed by a terrible skin infection, which afflicted people as well as the animals that had survived.

The natural world was in turmoil, reflecting the escalating spiritual conflict as each event exposed Pharaoh's refusal to recognize a higher authority. Some of the plagues directly challenged the creatures and concepts worshipped in Egypt, but it was the Pharaoh god-king who was seen to embody the life source of the nation around which the battle raged. His magicians could no longer replicate the demonstrations of God's power; his officials were beginning to recognize that Pharaoh could not protect them.

'Raised you up' (v. 16) may be better translated 'let you live'; once again God's patience and mercy are emphasized in the moment of judgment. The Bible is clear that all human political power stems from God and is subject to God—precisely the point that Jesus makes to Pilate: 'You would have no power over me if it were not given to you from above' (John 19:11).

Reflection

Pharaoh set himself against God's people (v. 17) and came up against God himself: 'If God is for us, who can be against us?' (Romans 8:31).

SR

25

Hard-hearted?

Then the Lord said to Moses, 'Go to Pharaoh, for I have hardened his heart and the hearts of his officials so that I may perform these signs of mine among them... and that you may know that I am the Lord.' So Moses and Aaron went to Pharaoh and said to him, '... If you refuse to let them go, I will bring locusts into your country tomorrow...' Pharaoh's officials said to him, 'How long will this man be a snare to us? Let the people go, so that they may worship the Lord their God. Do you not yet realize that Egypt is ruined?' ... Pharaoh said, '... No! Let only the men go and worship the Lord, since that's what you have been asking for.'

As the battle has raged, Pharaoh's behaviour has been increasingly consistent. At the height of each plague he is ready to submit. When the pressure is removed, however, he reinstates his stubborn refusal.

Does this not match your experience of human nature? When our very existence is threatened, it is easier to promise God total obedience than it is to keep the promise when we are living at ease, surrounded by temptation to put God back into the box we label 'only to be used in an emergency'. But we play a dangerous game. God is not at our beck and call.

Now the conflict has reached a new level. Pharaoh's stubbornness has become terminal: he has 'hardened his heart' so often that God has confirmed his decision. His advisers are now pleading with him to save the nation he is responsible for, but having turned his back on God he will not be swayed by mere mortals.

It is a dreadful reality that people can ultimately place themselves outside the scope of God's mercy—and the result is destruction. God's preferred business is the softening of hard hearts: 'I will... put a new spirit in them; I will remove from them their heart of stone and give them a heart of flesh... They will be my people, and I will be their God' (Ezekiel 11:19–20). Pharaoh, tragically, missed that opportunity and reached the point of no return.

Prayer

Merciful Father, keep me always open to you so that I may live in the confidence that you will never let me go.

SR

Light in the darkness

Then the Lord said to Moses, 'Stretch out your hand towards the sky so that darkness spreads over Egypt—darkness that can be felt.' … No one could see anyone else or move about for three days. Yet all the Israelites had light in the places where they lived. Then Pharaoh summoned Moses and said, 'Go, worship the Lord. Even your women and children may go with you; only leave your flocks and herds behind.' But Moses said, 'You must allow us to have sacrifices and burnt offerings to present to the Lord our God. Our livestock too must go with us…' But the Lord hardened Pharaoh's heart, and he was not willing to let them go.

'Darkness that can be felt.' The Hebrew is simply two words: it was 'dark dark'. It is amazing just how dark it can seem when the light is suddenly extinguished. Even in the most familiar of settings, we are forced to feel our way, full of uncertainty.

Some commentators suggest that this was probably a sandstorm, the sort that blacks out the sun in moments and fills the air with particles that get into everything. You certainly can feel this kind of darkness.

Moses and Pharaoh continue their Eastern-style bartering. Pharaoh had offered to let the men go; now he offers to allow the women and children—but he is not prepared to let go of everything. The wealth (the animals) have to stay. Notice that Moses wanted the animals to offer to God; Pharaoh wanted to keep them. It was another round of the same battle.

Light and darkness is one of the great biblical contrasts, often seen as parallel to life and death. 'God is light; in him there is no darkness at all,' says 1 John 1:5. Pharaoh's refusal to acknowledge God plunges his whole nation into darkness, while the people of God walk in the light.

The wonderful truth of God's offer of hope in and through Jesus is that he brings light—light to see the world as it really is, light to walk the path set before us, light that dispels all fear of the dark. Light also has the unerring ability to show up all the dirt. That's why Jesus' ability to clean up every stain is such good news.

Reflection

'In him was life, and that life was the light of all people' (John 1:4).

SR

The price is paid

Moses said, 'This is what the Lord says: "About midnight I will go throughout Egypt. Every firstborn son in Egypt will die, from the first-born son of Pharaoh, who sits on the throne, to the firstborn son of the female slave, who is at her hand mill, and all the firstborn of the cattle as well. There will be loud wailing throughout Egypt—worse than there has ever been or ever will be again. But among the Israelites not a dog will bark at any person or animal." Then you will know that the Lord makes a distinction between Egypt and Israel. All these officials of yours will come to me, bowing down before me and saying, "Go, you and all the people who follow you!" After that I will leave.' Then Moses, hot with anger, left Pharaoh.

It is awful. At first sight, this is not a reading to help you start the day with a spring in your step or end it ready for peaceful repose. It is a glimpse into monstrous suffering, terror and grief on an unbelievable scale. Even so, we must face it, and face what it tells us about God—and about the reality of sin.

This story tells me that 'God cannot be mocked. People reap what they sow' (Galatians 6:7). Pharaoh has enslaved a nation and slaughtered its male children as a matter of public policy; he has ignored God's offers of mercy as the warning signs have intensified. Now the dreadful price is to be paid.

I once read of a Hindu who became a Christian because in the Bible he discovered a God of justice, one who did not leave wickedness unpunished. This seems strange to our ears, possibly because we are rarely consistently oppressed and abused. Imagine if, day after day, you were on the receiving end of injustice that brought pain and suffering. You would long for God to do something.

God has done just that. Such is his love and mercy that he gave his own firstborn; such is his justice that his firstborn shed his own blood to pay the price of sin and let his people go free.

Prayer

Almighty God, grant me a deep longing for justice and a deep reserve of mercy. Amen

SR

EXODUS 12:1–11 (TNIV, ABRIDGED)

A ready meal

The Lord said to Moses and Aaron in Egypt, '... Tell the whole community of Israel that on the tenth day of this month each man is to take a lamb for his family, one for each household... All the members of the community of Israel must slaughter them at twilight. Then they are to take some of the blood and put it on the sides and tops of the door-frames of the houses where they eat the lambs. That same night they are to eat the meat roasted over the fire, along with bitter herbs, and bread made without yeast... This is how you are to eat it: with your cloak tucked into your belt, your sandals on your feet and your staff in your hand. Eat it in haste; it is the Lord's Passover.'

The contrast could not be greater. One part of the land was visited with a terrible disaster; in the other there was a slaughter of a different kind. The Egyptians had no livestock left; the Israelites took their best and voluntarily sacrificed it. Its blood was to bring protection, while its meat was to provide a meal of sustenance and celebration: they were finally on the move.

I doubt if you have cooked a roast dinner while the car was being packed for a lengthy journey. It is a task that can't be hurried, yet there was no time to make bread with yeast. This was a meal laden with deep theological significance rather than a recipe for effective fast food.

It was to be eaten in haste, not savoured. All the Eastern traditions for culinary appreciation were flouted: shoes on, ready to go. What a powerful indicator of spiritual truth! The great moment of liberation was upon them; God was about to demonstrate his power to save. It was not the end of the story, though; it was the beginning of a new chapter.

The Israelites' new life was to be characterized by movement. They had to get out and leave the old behind; they had to step out in faith and travel into the unknown, following the path set by God. What was true for them is true for us, too.

Prayer

God of liberating power, grant that we may eat with you and be ready to move with you. Amen

SR

Remember

Then Moses summoned all the elders of Israel and said to them, 'Go at once and select the animals for your families and slaughter the Passover lamb. Take a bunch of hyssop, dip it into the blood in the basin and put some of the blood on the top and on both sides of the door-frame... When the Lord goes through the land to strike down the Egyptians, he will see the blood on the top and sides of the door-frame and will pass over that doorway... When you enter the land that the Lord will give you as he promised, observe this ceremony. And when your children ask you, "What does this ceremony mean to you?" then tell them, "It is the Passover sacrifice to the Lord..."'

The blood of the lamb, applied to the door (to symbolize the place where the private and the public meet?), was to bring salvation. Here is a basic truth of God's good news delivered as a graphic picture. John the Baptist underlined it when he greeted Jesus with the words, 'Look, the Lamb of God, who takes away the sin of the world' (John 1:29).

The significance of this moment was such that the instructions were not only given for a meal to be eaten in haste, but also for its anniversary celebration every year into the future. Even before the first lamb had given up its life, its future relatives were being given a role in God's plan.

How would the people, who were about to experience God's saving power as never before, remember what he had done for them? How would the next generations, who would live in the benefit of this moment long into the future, be taught and reminded? By reenacting the meal and having its every significance stated to all, so that all would remember.

How good is your memory? We are all prone to ups and downs in our relationship with God; and it's amazing how easily we can forget what God has done for us in the past. The better we are at remembering, though, the more likely we are to trust God again in the future. The Passover was not an empty ritual; it was an aide-memoire of practical significance.

Reflection
Are you ready and able to recall what God has done for you, should someone ask?

SR

EXODUS 12:29–32 (TNIV)

The terrible harvest

At midnight the Lord struck down all the firstborn in Egypt, from the firstborn of Pharaoh, who sat on the throne, to the firstborn of the prisoner, who was in the dungeon, and the firstborn of all the live-stock as well. Pharaoh and all his officials and all the Egyptians got up during the night, and there was loud wailing in Egypt, for there was not a house without someone dead. During the night Pharaoh summoned Moses and Aaron and said, 'Up! Leave my people, you and the Israelites! Go, worship the Lord as you have requested. Take your flocks and herds, as you have said, and go. And also bless me.'

Pharaoh's consistent refusal to acknowledge God's authority and submit to his will now reaps a terrible harvest. It is the cutting down of all regarded as most precious, all in whom hope and investment for the future are reserved. It is cat-astrophic, devastating and final. That's the reality of sin.

This is not intended as a trite theological point that skates over the reality of human suffering. The Bible is clear that everything awful is the result of rebellion against God. The death of every firstborn all through history is, in that sense, the result of sin. Paul is explicit: death entered the world through sin 'and in this way death came to all people' (Romans 5:12) —and death brings terrible grief and anguish.

I remember talking to a woman in the Philippines who had lost many of her children. As she told me how she had desperately tried to save the life of her youngest just a few weeks earlier, tears filled her eyes. It still hurt. She had bor-rowed money she could not afford so that the baby could be buried with dignity. Rich and poor alike experience the grief that provokes loud wailing.

I can't emphasize enough that the other side of this coin is that God was prepared to enter into this very experience so that the impact of sin and death could be ended. God 'did not spare his own Son, but gave him up for us all' (Romans 8:32). So, finally, the people are set free. Freedom always comes at a price.

Prayer

Lord God, help us to understand the impact of sin so as to fully appreci-ate all you have done through Jesus.

SR

Time to go

The Egyptians urged the people to hurry and leave the country. 'For otherwise,' they said, 'we will all die!' … The Israelites journeyed from Rameses to Sukkoth. There were about six hundred thousand men on foot, besides women and children. Many other people went up with them, and also large droves of livestock, both flocks and herds. With the dough the Israelites had brought from Egypt, they baked loaves of unleavened bread. The dough was without yeast because they had been driven out of Egypt and did not have time to prepare food for themselves. Now the length of time the Israelite people lived in Egypt was 430 years. At the end of the 430 years, to the very day, all the Lord's divisions left Egypt.

It was the end of an era. At last this massive exodus, this great movement of people began. While the experts argue about the exact length of time and the exact size of the crowd—there are difficulties in harmonizing different Bible verses here—we can be absolutely certain that it was a defining moment of history.

Note a hint of 'prophetic' history in this reading. At this great moment of separation, when the people of God are released and leave the people and place of slavery behind, the division is not as clear-cut as one might expect. 'Many other people went up with them' (v. 38) and, in the years ahead, the descendants of this group caused Israel significant problems (for example, in Numbers 11).

Of course it was great, and completely understandable, that so many took the opportunity to make a break for freedom alongside the Israelite people. But while we need to encourage as many as possible to travel with us as we walk with God, as individuals and churches we may face difficulties if we allow undue space and influence to people and practices from our old lives that are not completely committed to God.

It is easy, on the one hand, to become isolationist and exclusive and, on the other, to become so absorbed in the ways of the world as to be indistinguishable from it. Either way, we lose our ability to be the salt and light of God's influence in the world.

Prayer

As I journey with you, Lord, help me to know what to leave behind and who to encourage to walk with me.

SR

EXODUS 13:1–3, 8–9 (TNIV)

A sign and reminder

The Lord said to Moses, 'Consecrate to me every firstborn male. The first offspring of every womb among the Israelites belongs to me, whether human or animal.' Then Moses said to the people, 'Commemorate this day, the day you came out of Egypt, out of the land of slavery, because the Lord brought you out of it with a mighty hand. Eat nothing containing yeast... On that day tell your children, "I do this because of what the Lord did for me when I came out of Egypt." This observance will be for you like a sign on your hand and a reminder on your forehead that this law of the Lord is to be on your lips. For the Lord brought you out of Egypt with his mighty hand.'

The exodus is not the end of the story. Of course it is significant—God has moved in power to set his people free—but why had Moses asked Pharaoh for release? So that the people could worship God. Worship was not just the performance of religious ritual; it was a life of service—and it still is. To use a cliché as true as it is old: we are saved to serve.

The firstborn of Egypt had died in the final act of judgment; the firstborn of Israel were to live lives of sacrifice to God, as a public sign and reminder to everyone of God's rightful expectation of them all. The festival of unleavened bread was the sign of a new start. It was an integral part of the Passover, but went on for seven days, showing that God's act of a moment has impact for ever (seven days being a symbol of completeness).

On the basis of this passage, by the time of Jesus, devout Jews had passages of the Law tied to their wrists and their foreheads (in phylacteries). Carrying out a religious ritual, however, is always easier than living out the symbolism. In their new life, every action and every thought had to be guided by God, the one who had saved them so that they could serve him. I hope that these words today have been to you a sign and a reminder. We all need them.

Reflection

We serve God because of who he is and what he has done; but then he does what he does because of who he is.

SR

I am with you always

Moses took the bones of Joseph with him because Joseph had made the Israelites swear an oath. He had said, 'God will surely come to your aid, and then you must carry my bones up with you from this place.' After leaving Sukkoth they camped at Etham on the edge of the desert. By day the Lord went ahead of them in a pillar of cloud to guide them on their way and by night in a pillar of fire to give them light, so that they could travel by day or night. Neither the pillar of cloud by day nor the pillar of fire by night left its place in front of the people.

For four hundred years the mummified remains of Joseph had been kept among the people, and with them the story of Joseph's final demand—that he should leave Egypt with them. Despite his power and his success, Joseph did not regard Egypt as home. What's more, he knew that God would intervene and take his people home. I wonder how much store was placed on Joseph's confidence in God when the days seemed darkest? But what a legacy he left—an unshakeable confidence in God's faithfulness! There are worse things we can leave to the generations to come.

Joseph's ancient experience of God was reinforced by the very up-to-date, visible presence of God (vv. 21–22). Was this God's recognition that a nation worn down by oppression and slavery needed every support as they set out into the unknown? Whenever they looked out of their tents, day or night, they knew that God was with them.

We need such confidence ourselves. Every day is in one sense an unknown to us; some days seem scarier than others, but whether we have set out on the journey of being a Christian or started a new job or moved to a new area—God is with us.

What's more, he is always ahead of us. The pillar of cloud and fire was a sign of God's leading and an assurance of God's protection. Sometimes we would love a physical sight of God, but we are called to walk by faith. Like Joseph, though, we have a promise: Jesus said, 'Surely I am with you always' (Matthew 28:20).

Prayer

Dear God, thank you for the assurance of your presence, day and night. Amen

SR

EXODUS 14:5–9 (TNIV)

Second thoughts—again

When the king of Egypt was told that the people had fled, Pharaoh and his officials changed their minds about them and said, 'What have we done? We have let the Israelites go and have lost their services!' So he had his chariot made ready and took his army with him. He took six hundred of the best chariots, along with all the other chariots of Egypt, with officers over all of them. The Lord hardened the heart of Pharaoh king of Egypt, so that he pursued the Israelites, who were marching out boldly. The Egyptians—all Pharaoh's horses and chariots, horsemen and troops—pursued the Israelites and overtook them as they camped by the sea near Pi Hahiroth, opposite Baal Zephon.

Pharaoh has not learned anything. The sound of wailing has barely died away, the speed with which the Israelites have been ushered out of Egypt forgotten. Suddenly there is another reality: no more slaves. The whole society will have to come to terms with doing its own work, unless… Egypt is a mighty military power: now is the time to use force.

It's the same story when Paul is in Philippi. A slave girl is set free from an evil spirit by the power of God, and her owners realize that their hope of exploiting her further for financial gain has gone. So they turn on Paul and Silas and get them thrown into jail (Acts 16). The fury of the powerful when their power is denied is terrible to behold.

Praise God, though, that when he intervenes in people's lives there is change that can be noticed! When revival came to Wales in 1905, one sign of changed lives was that the pit ponies were unable to move because swear words no longer formed part of the miners' commands.

More worrying are the societies seen to be full of churchgoers where nothing seems to change, where violence is seen as a legitimate weapon of power, where worship on Sunday exists alongside injustice, week in, week out. Where are the Christian whistle-blowers, those who challenge their companies to behave ethically? There will be times when those who serve God should shake the foundations of the world of the powerful.

Prayer

Lord God, enable all who follow you to know when—and how—to stand for you, whatever the cost.

SR

Stand firm

As Pharaoh approached, the Israelites looked up, and there were the Egyptians, marching after them. They were terrified and cried out to the Lord. They said to Moses, 'Was it because there were no graves in Egypt that you brought us to the desert to die? What have you done to us by bringing us out of Egypt? Didn't we say to you in Egypt, "Leave us alone; let us serve the Egyptians"? It would have been better for us to serve the Egyptians than to die in the desert!' Moses answered the people, 'Do not be afraid. Stand firm and you will see the deliverance the Lord will bring you today. The Egyptians you see today you will never see again. The Lord will fight for you; you need only to be still.'

Before we rush to judgment on the Israelites, we should consider their situation. Their world has been turned upside down, very rapidly. They longed for change, but they feel a very real sense of frying-pan and fire as they see the crack troops of the world's finest fighting machine zeroing in on them, trapping them between the desert and the sea. Rapid change and impending violence can all too easily create fear, and fear all too easily undermines confidence in God.

This mirrors the experience of many Christians—bold to follow God in the comfort zone of church; terrified to let those Monday morning work colleagues know where Sunday morning had been spent. Eager to seize the benefits of all that God has done; less willing to pay the price in lost friends or to face the reality of the battle in which every Christian is an enlisted soldier.

In many societies today, becoming a Christian brings the threat of physical violence. Some do turn back, fearful for themselves and their families, but many more would testify that they have stood firm and seen the deliverance of the Lord.

Moses' rallying cry was the truth we all need to hear from time to time: 'The Lord will fight for you.' We may lack the courage, the weapons and the training, just as those Israelites did. Yet when we can do nothing, we are asked to be still and let God fight for us—and he will.

Reflection

The battle belongs to the Lord.

SR

Deliverance

Moses stretched out his hand over the sea, and at daybreak the sea went back to its place. The Egyptians were fleeing towards it, and the Lord swept them into the sea. The water flowed back and covered the chariots and horsemen—the entire army of Pharaoh that had followed the Israelites into the sea. Not one of them survived. But the Israelites went through the sea on dry ground, with a wall of water on their right and on their left. That day the Lord saved Israel from the hands of the Egyptians, and Israel saw the Egyptians lying dead on the shore. And when the Israelites saw the great power the Lord displayed against the Egyptians, the people feared the Lord and put their trust in him and in Moses his servant.

This is one of the best-known Bible stories and one of the most dramatic. Moses stretches out his hand and God creates a path through the water for the Israelites. Moses stretches out his hand again and the Egyptian army is buried under the water. The greatest military might of the time has been swept aside in minutes. This is the moment when the people really know they are free.

Experts want to spend time debating whether this was the Red Sea or the Reed Sea, which is linked to the attempt to suggest a natural phenomenon that could offer a clear route for an enormous crowd and then, in no time, become a raging torrent. The Bible account is clearly about a supernatural event, one in which God so clearly demonstrated his power that people who had already seen the ten signs of his power expressed in the plagues were now ready to believe.

Nothing will convince us about God more than deliverance from our greatest fear and our greatest oppression. Praise God for every story of the power of addiction being broken. Praise God for every new believer who stands against the threat of violence from their community. Praise God for every time you have looked to him and he has not failed you.

The Israelites set out into their new future following the God who redeems, who saves, who delivers. So can we.

Prayer

Lord, you have acted in power in the past. Knowing this, we trust you for the future. Amen

SR

Stewards of creation

Our relationship with creation is a topical subject. Controversies rage about the reality and scale of global warming, about the least damaging ways of making use of the earth's resources for our human needs, about the best ways of generating energy and disposing of rubbish.

'Stewardship' is the most common contemporary Christian description of how we should relate to God's creation. It is undoubtedly a better way than that of 'dominion' —seeing everything else in creation as made for our benefit, to be used as we see fit. Both theologians and environmentalists have come to see disadvantages in the idea of stewardship, however, as summarized by Richard Mabey:

The problem with stewardship is not the guaranteeing of our share, but the belief that we also have the right, or the duty, to determine every other species' share too. The custodial relationship is intrinsically one of 'us' and 'them'. It assumes divisions, by power and importance, in a system that we know we must learn to see as a whole. (*Nature Cure*, Pimlico, 2006, p.109)

St Francis and St Clare offered an alternative eight centuries ago, which is still relevant today. They saw the system as a whole, created by the one Father, with everything as brother and sister to each other and therefore equal in power and importance. Paul expresses it in more theological terms when he writes that 'through [Christ] God was pleased to reconcile to himself all things' (Colossians 1:20).

This topic calls for change in heart and in lifestyle, so I want to suggest a few ways in which you might inform yourself for action after this coming fortnight. Christian Ecology Link produces a wide range of material. One suggestion is to use our LOAF when buying food—to look for food that is Locally produced, Organically grown, Animal friendly, and/or Fairly traded. Contact 3 Bond Street, Lancaster LA1 3ER or www.christian-ecology.org.uk.

A Rocha International (see http://en.arocha.org) has recently launched a simple commitment based on Psalm 24:1 (see 30 September reading), covering believing, behaving and belonging in response to the recognition that 'the earth is the Lord's'. Also, www.eco-congregation.org provides resources for churches to help them weave environmental issues into their life and mission, including a DIY environmental check-up.

Helen Julian CSF

All things come from thee

The earth is the Lord's and all that is in it, the world, and those who live in it; for he has founded it on the seas, and established it on the rivers. Who shall ascend the hill of the Lord? And who shall stand in his holy place? Those who have clean hands and pure hearts, who do not lift up their souls to what is false, and do not swear deceitfully. They will receive blessing from the Lord, and vindication from the God of their salvation.

Franciscans, following their founder St Francis, are well known for their love of nature, but it isn't a universal trait. I have one sister who prefers to appreciate creation through the windscreen of a car and another who isn't really happy unless her feet are on tarmac.

They would probably both say that people are more important than nature, and perhaps that's a good corrective to a form of 'nature worship' that ignores the place of humanity. Of course, ideally, we need to balance both these ingredients.

Francis didn't, in the end, love creation for its own sake, but because of his even greater love for the Creator. He saw signs of God's love and provision everywhere in creation, so appreciating nature led him to a greater appreciation of God, and his response to this appreciation was heartfelt worship.

He would have felt at home with the singers of the psalms in Old Testament times. Psalm 24, which was recited by the people at the beginning of their worship on the first day of the week, set the tone for all that followed. It may have been used at the procession of the ark of the covenant into the sanctuary (2 Samuel 6:12–15). It speaks of God as the universal Creator, very different from the local gods who had been worshipped in Jerusalem by the Jebusites, who lived there before it became the 'city of David'.

Those who are worthy to worship him are those who choose to act in accordance with God's will, recognizing his call on their obedience. They know that 'the earth is the Lord's', not theirs, and base their actions on that realization.

Reflection

'All things come from thee, and of thine own do we give unto thee'
(Book of Common Prayer).
How does this attitude affect your worship?

HJ CSF

Made in God's image

Then God said, 'Let us make humankind in our image, according to our likeness; and let them have dominion over the fish of the sea, and over the birds of the air, and over the cattle, and over all the wild animals of the earth, and over every creeping thing that creeps upon the earth.' So God created humankind in his image, in the image of God he created them; male and female he created them. God blessed them, and God said to them, 'Be fruitful and multiply, and fill the earth and subdue it; and have dominion over the fish of the sea and over the birds of the air and over every living thing that moves upon the earth.'

This text, from towards the end of the first Genesis account of the creation, marks a change in gear. Until now, each new day has been heralded with 'Let there be…'; from this point a more personal note comes in with 'Let us make…'. There is another change of gear, too. This is the first appearance of a hierarchical relationship between different parts of creation. Until now, each part of creation has been called into existence simply for its own sake. Here, humankind is made in God's image and likeness, given 'dominion' over all the other creatures and told to 'subdue' the earth.

Obviously this is a foundational text for any theology of our relationship with creation, and some people have come to see it as a problem. Professor Lynn White Jr of the University of California wrote a seminal article in the journal *Science*

in 1967, called 'The historical roots of our ecological crisis'. He traced the crisis (which was causing serious concern to some even then) to the victory of Christianity over paganism in medieval Europe and the triumph of the view, derived from this passage, that humanity was made to conquer nature, which had been made for its benefit.

This view does, of course, ignore other strands in biblical teaching, which stress our complete dependence on God and the fragility of our lives (see, for example, Job 4:17–19; Psalm 39:4–6; Isaiah 40:6–8). We should hear it, though, as a challenge to look critically at our tradition and at how we use it.

Reflection

How do different parts of the biblical tradition inform my relationship with creation?

HJ CSF

God's gardeners

In the day that the Lord God made the earth and the heavens, when no plant of the field was yet in the earth and no herb of the field had yet sprung up... the Lord God formed man from the dust of the ground, and breathed into his nostrils the breath of life; and the man became a living being. And the Lord God planted a garden in Eden, in the east; and there he put the man whom he had formed... The Lord God took the man and put him in the garden of Eden to till it and keep it.

We have moved on one chapter in the first book of the Bible and already there is a different image of the relationship between humankind and the earth. Here there is no mention of 'subduing' or of 'dominion'. Instead the man is given a necessary but humble job—tilling and keeping the earth that God has created, and in particular the garden, the part that is to provide what he needs for life.

I'm no gardener, but from watching gardeners I can see that tilling a garden is absorbing, requiring a close attention to what's happening. It is often hard work physically: nature keeps asserting itself and, without that regular work, will simply take over. It's also very satisfying, as things that have been nurtured grow and give pleasure through their beauty, and perhaps also as food.

The garden of Eden is often equated with paradise, with the ideal God-given environment, so it is interesting to see that paradise isn't incompatible with work. The word 'keep' obviously means 'tend' and 'care for', but in Hebrew it also means 'to guard' (Genesis 3:24). Maybe this isn't so far from 'dominion' as it might seem. The Hebrew word *radah*, which is translated 'dominion' (1:28), has the basic sense of 'to wander around' and is related to 'accompany, pasture and guide'. In my mind this begins to sound like a shepherd's work and, as Christians, we have the supreme example of Jesus, who laid down his life for the sheep. Our 'dominion' is to be as a shepherd to sheep, not as a despot using the land for our whims.

Prayer

*Creator God, help me to see where
I am called to shepherd
your creation today.*

HJ CSF

Universal sabbath

The Lord spoke to Moses on Mount Sinai, saying: Speak to the people of Israel and say to them: When you enter the land that I am giving you, the land shall observe a sabbath for the Lord. For six years you shall sow your field, and for six years you shall prune your vineyard, and gather in their yield; but in the seventh year there shall be a sabbath of complete rest for the land, a sabbath for the Lord: you shall not sow your field or prune your vineyard. You shall not reap the aftergrowth of your harvest or gather the grapes of your unpruned vine: it shall be a year of complete rest for the land.

The idea of sabbath runs through the Bible like a fine but glittering thread. From the weekly sabbath laid down by God through Moses (Exodus 20:8–11) to the jubilee year, the fiftieth year, of complete rest and complete liberation, which is described later in this chapter of Leviticus, it speaks of a relationship between God, his creation and the people made in his image that is more than purely functional.

The weekly sabbath of God's people speaks of a life that is more than just work, production and consumption—and the sabbath for the land is perhaps a way of demonstrating that the land also has its needs. It cannot simply be worked and expected to produce every year without a break.

The sabbath for the land is commanded twice, for two different reasons. In Exodus 23:10–11 the land is to be left fallow in the seventh year 'so that the poor of your people may eat'. In this passage from Leviticus, the reasons are theological: 'for the Lord'. As the people are to have their sabbath each week, on which they do not work but can focus on worship, so is the land to have one year in seven. It's unlikely that this sabbath ever took place exactly as it is laid down here, with the whole land resting in the same year, but the principle is a sound one. The land is worthy of respect and care. It is another way of recognizing that 'the earth is the Lord's'.

Reflection

How do I honour the principle of sabbath in my own life and in my use of the resources of the earth?

HJ CSF

LEVITICUS 25:18–23 (NRSV)

God's land, God's provision

You shall observe my statutes and faithfully keep my ordinances, so that you may live on the land securely. The land will yield its fruit, and you will eat your fill and live on it securely. Should you ask, 'What shall we eat in the seventh year, if we may not sow or gather in our crop?' I will order my blessing for you in the sixth year, so that it will yield a crop for three years. When you sow in the eighth year, you will be eating from the old crop; until the ninth year, when its produce comes in, you shall eat the old. The land shall not be sold in perpetuity, for the land is mine; with me you are but aliens and tenants.

One of the provisions for the year of jubilee, of which this passage forms part, was that the land should be returned to its original owners. If it was sold during the time between jubilee years, it was not sold in perpetuity, but only for the number of years until the next jubilee. In effect, the buyer was buying a number of crops, not the land itself.

This is a very different system from that used in most Western countries, where money and ownership are absolute values, but it is reflected in many more traditional cultures, such as the native peoples of North America. 'The earth does not belong to us; we belong to the earth,' said Chief Seattle, and Richard Mabey writes, '… a belief that land is a kind of common inheritance is deep-rooted, and may be there instinctively from the beginning of life' (*Nature Cure*, p. 120).

This way of living raises real practical questions, however, which God's people are not afraid to voice. On what are an agricultural people to live if they are not to sow or gather every seventh year? They have no freezers full of supplies, no foreign imports of food. Instead they must put their trust in God and in God's provision for them. The covenant that God has made with them makes demands on them, but also promises God's care for them. If they keep what is commanded, then God will give them security.

Reflection

Do I really believe that God will supply my needs if I keep my covenant with him?

HJ CSF

Holy stewards

But if, despite this, you disobey me, and continue hostile to me, I will continue hostile to you in fury; I in turn will punish you myself sevenfold for your sins... I will devastate the land, so that your enemies who come to settle in it shall be appalled at it. And you I will scatter among the nations, and I will unsheathe the sword against you; your land shall be a desolation, and your cities a waste. Then the land shall enjoy its sabbath years as long as it lies desolate, while you are in the land of your enemies; then the land shall rest, and enjoy its sabbath years.

If there are rewards in keeping God's covenant, there are also consequences if it is not kept. In the Old Testament, both the blessings of obedience and the curses of disobedience are often seen in material terms. This passage comes at the end of the 'holiness code', a long passage in the book of Leviticus from 17:1 to 26:46. It is a sermon, setting before the people both the way of life and the way of destruction. Many of its provisions are very specific and some now seem strange, such as not sowing fields with two different kinds of seed or wearing garments made of two different materials (19:19). The overriding concern of the author, however, is for the holiness of God's people, demonstrated by their willingness not just to keep each little law but to follow God's ways as a whole.

How is this linked to our stewardship of creation? A steward is the agent of another, and traditionally the 'other' is the landowner. For Christians, the 'other' is, of course, God. A good steward sees his or her role as acting in the way in which the owner would act if present.

So we are to take our cue as stewards, made in God's image, from the way in which God exercises power. We are not stewards for our own benefit, but are to care for creation in the way that God does—wisely and benevolently.

This is the holiness that the code in Levicitus demands of us and it is as relevant today as it was then.

Reflection

How would I treat creation differently if I saw myself as this kind of steward?

HJ CSF

Judgment from God

What the cutting locust left, the swarming locust has eaten. What the swarming locust left, the hopping locust has eaten, and what the hopping locust left, the destroying locust has eaten... Alas for the day! For the day of the Lord is near, and as destruction from the Almighty it comes. Is not the food cut off before our eyes, joy and gladness from the house of our God? The seed shrivels under the clods, the storehouses are desolate; the granaries are ruined because the grain has failed. How the animals groan! The herds of cattle wander about because there is no pasture for them; even the flocks of sheep are dazed.

The name of the prophet Joel means 'Yahweh is God' and his message is one of the supremacy and power of God. He is writing during a great locust plague, which he sees as both present judgment from God and a symbol of the final day of the Lord, the last judgment.

Locusts were an ever-present reality for the people of Israel; there are nine different Hebrew words for locusts at different stages of their lives and four of them are found here—cutting, swarming, hopping and destroying. Just the names give a vivid picture of the destruction they brought, devouring everything in their path. Normal life came to an end and it was impossible to celebrate the usual feasts at the temple in Jerusalem.

'Joy and gladness' were especially associated with four feasts in the book of Deuteronomy: peace offerings (12:7), the presentation of the first fruits (26:10–11), the feast of Weeks (16:11) and the feast of Tabernacles (16:14–15). The inability to celebrate would have brought home to the people the seriousness of God's displeasure with them.

What might our equivalent be today? What will bring home to us the seriousness of our failure to be good stewards of God's creation? Will it be the hosepipe ban, the increased price of staple vegetables because of lack of rain, the rising tides and crumbling coastline at our favourite holiday resort, the dwindling numbers of our favourite wild bird? We must read the signs of the times as the people of Joel's day did when the locusts came, and turn back to God as they did.

Prayer

*God of creation, forgive us
our carelessness.*

HJ CSF

Brothers and sisters

If you come on a bird's nest, in any tree or on the ground, with fledglings or eggs, with the mother sitting on the fledglings or on the eggs, you shall not take the mother with the young. Let the mother go, taking only the young for yourself, in order that it may go well with you, and you may live long... You shall not muzzle an ox while it is treading out the grain... The righteous know the needs of their animals, but the mercy of the wicked is cruel.

Today is Animal Welfare Sunday, although this little collection of scattered verses demonstrates that the Bible does not say much about animal welfare as such. In a subsistence economy, domestic animals are a necessary part of existence, but they are expected to fulfil their purpose of providing labour or food. There is little room for sentimentality.

These passages, however, scattered though they are, do show that the proper treatment of both domestic and wild animals was a concern. Animals were not seen purely in functional terms. Interestingly, the verses from Deuteronomy come from a part of the chapter that is concerned mainly with the welfare of others. 'Others', therefore, are not seen purely in human terms. There is a sense of interdependence, that the animals, domestic and wild, have their place and their needs and their right to respectful treatment. Especially in the first passage,

there is a careful balance between human needs and respect for nature. We need food, so it is acceptable to take the eggs or the young birds. To take the mother bird as well is short-sighted, however, trading in a larger immediate meal for the future promise of more eggs and young birds in years to come.

Even without seeing the birds and animals as our brothers and sisters, as St Francis did, it is simply good stewardship to treat them well so as to meet our own needs. But the possibility is there for a deeper sense of equality, a recognition of fellowship in our created nature, of being all children of the one Father, and therefore in truth brother and sister to one another.

Reflection

How have I made use of animals this week? Have I respected their rights as well as my needs?

HJ CSF

JOB 38:1, 25–27; 39:5–7 (NRSV)

A broader perspective

Then the Lord answered Job out of the whirlwind:... 'Who has cut a channel for the torrents of rain, and a way for the thunderbolt, to bring rain on a land where no one lives, on the desert, which is empty of human life, to satisfy the waste and desolate land, and to make the ground put forth grass? ... 'Who has let the wild ass go free? Who has loosed the bonds of the swift ass, to which I have given the steppe for its home, the salt land for its dwelling place? It scorns the tumult of the city; it does not hear the shouts of the driver.'

Whose interests do we have at heart when we care for the earth? Much of our stewardship is, if we're honest, for our own benefit. We don't want the earth's resources to run out when it will mean changing the way we live, or the climate to change if it will affect our own country. At best, perhaps, we will make changes for the sake of our children and grandchildren.

Richard Mabey describes the attitude of most of us: 'Mainstream environmentalism is unashamedly utilitarian and human-centred. It's based on enlightened self-interest: we want a healthy, unpolluted, species-rich ecosystem because our material future depends on it' (*Nature Cure*, p. 109).

This anthropocentric view is not wrong, but it's not enough—and there's always the danger that our stewardship will slip into managing the world for our benefit rather than caring for it as God cares for it.

This passage is a corrective. Job has spent 37 chapters lamenting his lot (with every justification) and seeking answers from God. Now God does answer, but not in the way that Job expected. Instead, Job is offered a fresh perspective: not everything has been made for our benefit. God sends rain on uninhabited lands for their own sake and has created animals that do not serve our needs but only their own. The creation is good in its own terms; indeed, in Genesis 1 God sees that it is good before people have been created. That sense of the independence of nature, its existence on its own terms and in its own right, is the lesson of today's reading.

Prayer
Loving God, today I rejoice in all of your creation.

HJ CSF

Daily bread, daily choice

God said, 'See, I have given you every plant yielding seed that is upon the face of all the earth, and every tree with seed in its fruit; you shall have them for food. And to every beast of the earth, and to every bird of the air, and to everything that creeps on the earth, everything that has the breath of life, I have given every green plant for food.' And it was so... God blessed Noah and his sons, and said to them, 'Be fruitful and multiply and fill the earth... Every moving thing that lives shall be food for you; and just as I gave you the green plants, I give you everything.'

People often assume that Franciscans must all be vegetarians. In fact, we're not, although some do make that choice; one or two are even vegan. Francis himself was not vegetarian. He told his first brothers to eat what was set in front of them, seeing it as being part of poverty not to reject the food that was offered.

The choices we make about our food are a daily part of our stewardship. We don't often have to make decisions about a new car or flying to the other side of the world, but every day we have to eat.

The biblical evidence, in which these two passages are key, is not unambiguous. Some see the Genesis 1 passage as symbolic, a picture of what life was like in Eden and will be again in the kingdom of God. The famous passage from Isaiah 11:6–9, 'The wolf shall live with the lamb...', is another vivid picture of the same coming kingdom. These interpreters would see the second Genesis passage, in which humans are allowed to eat animals as well as plants, as a recognition of the fallen state of things.

Others would see the Genesis 1 passage as how things were created to be. Humans and animals share the same table and the human right of dominion is significantly limited. Then the passage from Genesis 9 marks a much more cataclysmic change. Now violence and killing are widespread, and the intended relationship between humanity and the rest of creation has been severely disrupted.

Which interpretation will you choose to follow?

Reflection

How do the choices I make about food reflect my understanding of creation?

HJ CSF

A rich fool

Then [Jesus] told them a parable: 'The land of a rich man produced abundantly. And he thought to himself, "What should I do, for I have no place to store my crops?" Then he said, "I will do this: I will pull down my barns and build larger ones, and there I will store all my grain and my goods. And I will say to my soul, Soul, you have ample goods laid up for many years; relax, eat, drink, be merry." But God said to him, "You fool! This very night your life is being demanded of you. And the things you have prepared, whose will they be?" So it is with those who store up treasures for themselves but are not rich towards God.'

This parable of Jesus, told in the context of a family dispute over property, seems at first sight to have little to do with stewardship of creation. In fact, though, it is a vivid demonstration of an attitude that is the polar opposite of being a good steward.

The rich man lives in a world bounded only by his own needs and his own choices. Faced with the quandary of an over-abundance of crops, he doesn't talk to anyone else and doesn't contemplate sharing his abundance with others. His conversation is all with himself and full of possessive pronouns, of 'I' and 'my'. He believes that his soul can be satisfied with material wealth.

God cuts straight to the heart of the matter when he addresses him as 'You fool!' It is not the sinfulness of wealth that is at stake here, but its futility. All the wealth that we can create and amass and protect is only temporary. As the old saying has it, there are no pockets in shrouds. If we create and sustain our identity on the basis of what we have, we can only end up disappointed and at a loss.

If, instead, we see what we have as held in trust—to be used for our own needs, yes, but also for the needs of others, and to be acquired with care for the real costs to the earth and to our fellow human beings—then what we have cannot be lost.

Reflection

Is my identity built on what I have or on who I am?

HJ CSF

Parables from creation

[Jesus said] 'Listen! A sower went out to sow. And as he sowed, some seed fell on the path, and the birds came and ate it up. Other seed fell on rocky ground, where it did not have much soil, and it sprang up quickly, since it had no depth of soil. And when the sun rose, it was scorched; and since it had no root, it withered away. Other seed fell among thorns, and the thorns grew up and choked it, and it yielded no grain. Other seed fell into good soil and brought forth grain, growing up and increasing and yielding thirty and sixty and a hundredfold.'

The sower in this parable of Jesus might seem to have been rather careless. Surely if he had made sure that all the seed fell into the ploughed ground in the first place, the harvest would have been better?

In Jesus' homeland, sowing came before ploughing. The path would have been ploughed up after the sowing. Perhaps the birds knew that this was their chance and got in quickly. In any case, the story shows us that Jesus knew the farmers' ways. Maybe as a boy he had been employed to scare the birds away until the ground was ploughed and the seed safely in the ground?

Jesus often uses natural imagery in his parables and other teaching: not just seed (Matthew 13:24–32) but also fishing (vv. 47–50), trees (Luke 6:43–45), birds and flowers (12:22–31). He noticed what was around him, what were the everyday concerns of the people to whom he was speaking, and used pictures that would be vivid for them.

Perhaps nowadays we need to be thinking of ways of talking about God and the kingdom that use the imagery of cars and computers? I think we do, but the imagery of the created world, of which we are also a part, is still powerful and still speaks to people. Part of our stewardship of creation is to be noticing the tiny details and small delights of nature, primarily to increase our own sense of wonder and gratitude to God, but also so that we can share with others in a way that might lead them into that wonder and gratitude.

Prayer

God of creation, teach me today through your creation.

HJ CSF

All things in Christ

[Christ] is the image of the invisible God, the firstborn of all creation; for in him all things in heaven and on earth were created, things visible and invisible, whether thrones or dominions or rulers or powers— all things have been created through him and for him. He himself is before all things, and in him all things hold together. He is the head of the body, the church; he is the beginning, the firstborn from the dead, so that he might come to have first place in everything. For in him all the fullness of God was pleased to dwell, and through him God was pleased to reconcile to himself all things, whether on earth or in heaven, by making peace through the blood of his cross.

'In the beginning...': the opening words of Genesis and of John's Gospel are the key to this passage. Paul makes the amazing claim that Christ is the beginning. This is a strong word, meaning not just the point at which things happen to have begun, but the first principle, the source.

When God created the heavens and the earth, Christ was already there. He is sometimes identified with divine wisdom (1 Corinthians 1:24) and in Proverbs 8 Wisdom speaks: 'The Lord created me at the beginning of his work... When he established the heavens, I was there' (see vv. 22, 27). So although Christ, the word and the wisdom of God, became incarnate as Jesus at a particular time in order to work our redemption, he was also intimately involved with the creation of the whole world. This is one of the reasons why we cannot separate our own redemption from the redemption of the world. We are all in Christ and 'in him all things hold together'.

Christ is not only the beginning of creation, but also the beginning of new creation, the new life of the resurrection. As head of the body, the Church, he takes with him through death all who believe; as 'the beginning' he takes with him also everything that was created in him.

This incredibly rich passage ought to widen our horizons and strengthen our sense of identity with the created world, because Christ holds us all together.

Reflection

'All things' is repeated four times in this passage; what are you tempted to leave out of God's redemptive power?

HJ CSF

51

Return to the Lord

Do not fear, O soil; be glad and rejoice, for the Lord has done great things! Do not fear, you animals of the field, for the pastures of the wilderness are green; the tree bears its fruit, the fig tree and vine give their full yield. O children of Zion, be glad and rejoice in the Lord your God; for he has given the early rain for your vindication... The threshing-floors shall be full of grain, the vats shall overflow with wine and oil. I will repay you for the years that the swarming locust has eaten, the hopper, the destroyer, and the cutter, my great army, which I sent against you. You shall eat in plenty and be satisfied, and praise the name of the Lord your God, who has dealt wondrously with you.

Just as, a week ago, we saw how Joel used natural disaster as a sign of God's judgment, now we have a vivid picture of natural blessing and abundance as a sign of God's pleasure in his people.

The whole book of Joel goes into reverse here. From 1:1 to 2:11, all is disastrous: the locusts devour the crops, the granaries are empty, vines, figs and pomegranates dry up and wither, and both domestic and wild animals suffer because of the drought. Then comes the turning point: 'Yet even now, says the Lord, return to me with all your heart' (2:12). The people are called to repentance, to a real change of heart, and God has pity on them. The rains return, the locusts vanish, the granaries are full and the trees give abundant fruit.

It is a dramatic picture of the interdependence of the people and the land, and it is the land that is called on to rejoice first, before the children of Zion.

We may no longer be happy with a theology that sees natural disaster as a punishment from God, but we cannot escape the fact that our actions have consequences. The way we treat the world has an effect on the world and that in turn affects our lives and the lives of our children. If we are to fulfil our calling as stewards of creation, we need a renewed sense of our oneness with it in Christ.

Reflection

What one thing will you do differently as a result of this fortnight's readings?

HJ CSF

Profile of a prophet: Samuel

Samuel is a fascinating figure—one of the most subtly drawn in the Bible. Unusually, we see him in a range of situations: starting with his parents, Hannah and Elkanah, before he is born; as a child who hears God calling in the night; through his struggles as a prophet with Saul the king; as the respected old man anointing David. He interacts with some of the most striking characters in the Old Testament: his brave mother, Hannah; his predecessor as prophet, Eli, the father of troublesome sons; Saul, the depressive ruler, and keen young David.

Often, Samuel seems to be at the still centre of turbulent events, but he is not just a blank canvas on which other, more powerful people make their mark. It might seem as if he doesn't bring much to the party, but there is a great deal happening underneath the unruffled surface. He can call on God to produce thunder and rain out of season (1 Samuel 12:18) and is even 'in charge of' a company of prophets in a frenzy (19:20). He has the difficult job of guiding the people of Israel—of giving them God's message (which often they don't want to hear) and also of sticking by them even when they take a wrong turning (such as their desire for a king).

Samuel quietly carries out his duties, winning the respect of the people without taking bribes, while others—especially Saul—do the more dramatic business. He doesn't always understand God's plans (he is surprised at the choice of David as the new king), but he obeys none the less. He is not perfect: he can't control his wayward sons, for example. Yet all Israel mourns when he dies.

As with other Old Testament characters, we see both what to follow and what to avoid. We should be wary of seeing these figures as patterns simply to copy. We can learn something here from the Jewish attitude of looking at them as examples of good and bad mixed together, and not people to be wholly admired. One of the main points from Samuel's life helps us to rise above such judgments, however. It is that we don't have to be at the very centre of big, historic events to heed his message about the supreme need for faithfulness to God.

Rachel Boulding

Pouring out my soul before the Lord

[Hannah] made this vow: 'O Lord of hosts, if only you will look on the misery of your servant, and remember me, and not forget your servant, but will give to your servant a male child, then I will set him before you as a nazirite until the day of his death...' Hannah was praying silently; only her lips moved, but her voice was not heard; therefore Eli thought she was drunk. So Eli said to her, 'How long will you make a drunken spectacle of yourself? Put away your wine.' But Hannah answered, 'No, my lord... I have been pouring out my soul before the Lord.'

From the outside, we can only faintly imagine the depth of Hannah's misery. Being unable to do the one thing that she, and everyone around her, felt she was made for—having children—must have pushed her to the edge of despair. It might seem obvious to us, with hindsight, that such unhappiness would propel her to the Lord, to seek his help, but it isn't always so clear for those who are troubled. Many people are so smothered by misery that they don't even realize that they can turn to God. A counsellor writes of the many Christians who seek her help, who feel they can pray only when their problems have got better (Judy Hirst, *Struggling to be Holy*, DLT, 2006). This seems bizarre—like taking medicine after you've already recovered—but it shows how many of us are pushed by troubles into such damaging fears that we don't even know where to go for help.

Probably like many others today, Hannah had to be tough in defending herself in front of Eli. She might just have slunk away in shame under his false accusation. Instead, though, she lays claim on her position as a servant of God and isn't afraid to ask for what she wants. She doesn't just wallow in her misery, but does something about it. How often do we do this, failing to take Jesus' words to heart about asking our heavenly Father for what we need? If we ask for bread, will he give us a stone (Matthew 7:7–11)?

Prayer

God our Father, help us to turn to you in our troubles, and find the comfort that you are always ready to offer.

RB

The wicked shall be silent

And Hannah prayed, and said, My heart rejoiceth in the Lord... because I rejoice in thy salvation... The bows of the mighty men are broken, and they that stumbled are girded with strength... He raiseth up the poor out of the dust, and lifteth up the beggar from the dunghill, to set them among princes, and to make them inherit the throne of glory... He will keep the feet of his saints, and the wicked shall be silent in darkness; for by strength shall no man prevail.

God answers Hannah's prayer. She gives birth to a son and keeps her promise to dedicate him to the Lord. But this is more than a cold bargain. She radiates a deep gratitude and knows that her joy comes from God rather than any virtue of her own. The prayer of thanksgiving that she pours out is, of course, partly a model for Mary's Magnificat ('My soul doth magnify the Lord...' Luke 1:46–55).

Like the Magnificat, Hannah's prayer conveys a strong sense of God reversing the world's normal order of power. Usually, men rule with violence and physical threat, using resources accumulated in the past. God turns that on its head and breaks the bows of the mighty (v. 4), giving their possessions to those who will appreciate them. The people who were despised are given respect (v. 8), for it is God who has the real power.

He judges the wicked, 'for by strength shall no man prevail'. Humans never seem to learn this. We might feel that the judgment comes too slowly, and often only after suffering that seems too great to bear, but we must have faith that God will triumph in the end. Wars do finish; dictators do fall, and not everyone dies young. It's ironic that people in places where there are often such disasters seem to have less trouble seeing this than those of us in the affluent West. We hear of people worshipping faithfully and joyfully in African refugee camps, while those of us who have too much food and too many possessions cannot see how God is relevant.

For prayer

Father, grant that we may see the world as it truly is, undergirded by your love, rather than ruled by those with temporary power.

RB

A voice calling in the dark

Samuel was lying down in the temple of the Lord, where the ark of God was. Then the Lord called, 'Samuel! Samuel!' and he said, 'Here I am!' and ran to Eli, and said, 'Here I am, for you called me.' But he said, 'I did not call; lie down again.' So he went and lay down... The Lord called Samuel again, a third time. And he got up and went to Eli, and said, 'Here I am, for you called me.' Then Eli perceived that the Lord was calling the boy. Therefore Eli said to Samuel, 'Go, lie down; and if he calls you, you shall say, "Speak, Lord, for your servant is listening."'

We move on now to Samuel as a boy, serving in the temple. Here is one of the most vivid stories in the Bible—one that we can all relate to. There is something intrinsically moving about the idea of being woken in the night. We've all experienced it and the combination of befuddlement and vulnerability it brings. It's also a special time, when things come to us more vividly, free from the distractions of the day. We wonder if we are dreaming and what is really happening.

There is certainly this sense of 'not being with it' as Eli takes three tries to work out what is happening. He might have expected God to address him, as he was the prophet, rather than speaking to a mere child. The times when we are a bit dozy seem to be when God can break through our pride—particularly that sense we can have of being important and self-sufficient.

As Hannah's thanksgiving suggested, when these barriers are down, we're more open to God and have fewer distractions. God can use our vulnerability to remind us that his grace is sufficient (2 Corinthians 12:9) and also how impossible it is for us to achieve anything substantial on our own: 'Unless the Lord builds the house, those who build it labour in vain' (Psalm 127:1).

For reflection

Can you think of a time when you were tired, or perhaps ill, when God spoke to you in a more distinct way —when you were able to hear him better without other things getting in the way? Did this suggest anything to you about the barriers (such as busyness) that you might normally put up against God?

RB

1 Samuel 3:11–18 (NRSV, ABRIDGED)

When your children turn from God

Then the Lord said to Samuel, 'See, I am about to do something in Israel that will make both ears of anyone who hears of it tingle... I have told [Eli] that I am about to punish his house for ever, for the iniquity that he knew, because his sons were blaspheming God, and he did not restrain them...' Samuel was afraid to tell the vision to Eli. But... Eli said, 'What was it that he told you? Do not hide it from me...' So Samuel told him everything and hid nothing from him. Then he said, 'It is the Lord; let him do what seems good to him.'

In this story, we are often so fascinated by the way God speaks to Samuel that we often forget what the dire message is. When it comes, it's a tough one, about Eli's house being cut off from God because of the way they have been corrupt and unfaithful (see 1 Samuel 2:12–17). Samuel is understandably nervous about telling Eli, but in the end he gives it to him straight. Eli is wise and humble enough to know that he has done wrong in failing to discipline his sons, and he accepts God's judgment.

Our hearts go out to Eli. So many religious leaders, right up to the present day, have children who turn away from the Lord. Even when their dearest wish and fervent prayer is for their children to have the same relationship with God that has been the central point of their own lives—even then, their children reject God. Sometimes the rebellion is spectac-ular, as in the case of a vicar's son I heard about who ended up in prison.

It's something that everyone who professes a faith needs to watch out for, not just the leaders. This is definitely not to say that parents are at fault if their children don't become good Christians, but the rebellion of our children is something that we have to offer to God each day. Our families will always have the free choice to turn away from him. God will not force them into a relationship with him and neither can we. We have to trust God to bring his purposes about in his own good time.

For prayer

Offer to God whatever is on your heart about your family.

RB

God dwells in a thankful heart

Then Samuel said to all the house of Israel, 'If you are returning to the Lord with all your heart, then put away the foreign gods and the Astartes from among you. Direct your heart to the Lord, and serve him only, and he will deliver you...' The lords of the Philistines went up against Israel... The people of Israel said to Samuel, 'Do not cease to cry out to the Lord our God for us, and pray that he may save us from the hand of the Philistines.' ... Samuel cried out to the Lord for Israel, and the Lord answered him... Then Samuel took a stone... and named it Ebenezer; for he said, 'Thus far the Lord has helped us.'

Here we have a typical example of Samuel's activity as prophet. It seems straightforward on the surface: Samuel tells the people they have been wicked; they repent and turn back to God; God defeats the Philistines for them. But there are hints of something else. The Israelites get jittery and say something like, 'Carry on praying, and louder!' They're not sure whether they have been good enough for God to help them, or perhaps they even doubt that God *can* help them.

God does save them, however, and Samuel sets up a stone to commemorate the event. Perhaps he is worried that the Israelites might forget all this favour when they have got used to their victory. Isn't it amazing how quickly we get used to blessings, like nine of the ten lepers who were cured by Jesus (Luke 17:17)? Very soon, we take it for granted and forget how hard things used to be. We forget to be thankful for being saved from disaster—such as a life-threatening diagnosis or an accident that could have been so much worse.

We should be conscious of our dependence on God and cultivate thankfulness as an attitude of mind and heart. There's a saying about Christians not being any better or nicer than others—just more grateful. As Izaak Walton, the 17th-century writer, put it, 'God has two dwellings: one in heaven and the other in a thankful heart.'

Prayer

Father, may your gifts draw me back to you; may they not distract me with their delights, but push me back to the giver. Amen

RB

The people reject their true king

Yet [Samuel's] sons did not follow in his ways, but turned aside after gain; they took bribes and perverted justice. Then all the elders of Israel gathered together and came to Samuel at Ramah, and said to him, 'You are old and your sons do not follow in your ways; appoint for us, then, a king to govern us, like other nations.' But the thing displeased Samuel when they said, 'Give us a king to govern us.' Samuel prayed to the Lord, and the Lord said to Samuel, 'Listen to the voice of the people in all that they say to you; for they have not rejected you, but they have rejected me from being king over them.'

With a horrible human predictability, Samuel's sons turn to the bad in a similar way to the sons of Eli, who was prophet before him. This happens to us all in various ways: as we fail to learn the lessons of those around us, so we repeat patterns of sin. Isn't this just how sin works, worming its way in, suggesting that the bad is normal and the good is somehow odd? So Samuel's sons follow through the pattern, and Samuel, like Eli before him, suffers for it.

God is amazingly merciful, though. He doesn't condemn Samuel but sees the wider picture. From his perspective of eternity, he is able to get a truer and more loving sense of what is going on. So he is gracious to Samuel, taking the trouble to reassure him and explain the situation. Thus he breaks the cycle.

God is also gracious in a different way with the people of Israel. He knows that their motivation in asking for a king is that they think a king will be easier on them than God is. Like everyone else, they are after constant blessing, with no awkward duties attached. I remember a minister talking about a local church mission. After days of special events in the church, the place was packed with happy people, singing joyfully together. They came for the uplift. But after only a few weeks of jollity, the newcomers began to thin out. People fell away because they didn't want steady commitment. 'They just wanted the blessing,' said the minister.

For reflection

In what ways am I looking only for blessing from God?

RB

What do you wish for?

So Samuel reported all the words of the Lord to the people who were asking him for a king. He said, 'These will be the ways of the king who will reign over you: he will take your sons and appoint them to his chariots and to be his horsemen, and to run before his chariots... He will take your daughters to be perfumers and cooks and bakers. He will take the best of your fields and vineyards and olive orchards and give them to his officers and his courtiers. He will take... the best of your cattle and donkeys, and put them to his work. He will take one-tenth of your flocks, and you shall be his slaves. And in that day you will cry out because of your king, whom you have chosen for yourselves; but the Lord will not answer you in that day.'

God deals with the children of Israel straightforwardly. Unlike them, he is not petulant. He takes their request for a king seriously, and is prepared to give them what they want, if only he can give them a fair warning about it. Hence he tells Samuel to convey to them exactly what a king will mean. They can hardly say they were deceived. He is just like a good father, who will take the trouble to explain the consequences of an action. He treats them like adults, but they behave like children.

Could God have acted differently here? Should he have said to the children of Israel: 'Because I love you so much, I'm not going to allow you to be so stupid'? Yes, he could have done that, but that would have been to treat them like real babies, coercing them to follow him because he knew best. No father or mother wants a grudging slave; they want to win over their children's hearts and minds.

God gives Israel, and the rest of us, free will. He gives due warning about what will happen and tries to win round his people, now and in the future. It's rather like so many of God's dealings with us. Ideally, we wouldn't have started from here, but now that we have begun, it's up to us, with God's help, to make the best of it.

For reflection

Be careful what you wish for: God might take you seriously.

RB

'It's only me'

Saul [was] a handsome young man. There was not a man among the people of Israel more handsome than he; he stood head and shoulders above everyone else... When Samuel saw Saul, the Lord told him, 'Here is the man of whom I spoke to you. He it is who shall rule over my people.' ... [Samuel said to Saul] 'And on whom is all Israel's desire fixed, if not on you and on all your ancestral house?' Saul answered, 'I am only a Benjaminite, from the least of the tribes of Israel, and my family is the humblest of all the families of the tribe of Bemjamin. Why then have you spoken to me in this way?'

Here we have the first appearance of Saul, the man whom God chooses as king. It is clear that Saul has already been blessed by God, his height giving him advantage. Even today, surveys suggest that leaders in business and politics are usually taller than average (something that doesn't cheer a puny person like me, at all of five foot two).

Saul sets out on a journey in search of his father's lost donkeys (see the rest of this chapter). He is presented as being like a folktale hero, off on a quest and being drawn to a mysterious man, the prophet Samuel, who knows when to expect him. God is using all these circumstances to bring about his purpose.

Like many before and after him, Saul is rightly humble when faced with God's plans for him. He is like Isaiah ('I am a man of unclean lips...' Isaiah 6:5), David and many others, including Samuel himself—not quite believing that God is calling him. Of course, we are right to have the same attitude, but often we go too far, getting stuck in a debilitating false modesty. It's as if we never really believe that God can use us for anything. Well, he can and he does. Who are we to disagree? He might only be calling us today to help someone in need, perhaps in a very trivial way, with a kind word or an offer of tea, but our doubts about being able to do anything at all can get in the way.

For reflection

What small task is God calling you towards at worship this Sunday?

RB

God gave him another heart

Samuel took a phial of oil and poured it on [Saul's] head, and kissed him; he said, 'The Lord has anointed you ruler over his people Israel... Now this shall be the sign to you that the Lord has anointed you ruler over his heritage... you will meet a band of prophets coming down from the shrine with harp, tambourine, flute, and lyre playing in front of them; they will be in a prophetic frenzy. Then the spirit of the Lord will possess you, and you will be in a prophetic frenzy along with them and be turned into a different person...' As [Saul] turned away to leave Samuel, God gave him another heart; and all these signs were fulfilled that day.

Samuel, told by God that this is the new leader, now anoints Saul. To confirm Saul's position, Samuel also gives him signs from God, including people he will meet on the way back home, and possession by a prophetic frenzy. This is heady stuff, as is the fact that he will be 'turned into a different person', but God is firmly in control. This is rule under God's authority, as Samuel anoints him merely to be 'ruler' or 'prince', rather than king. Scholars also question the translation that refers to Saul's 'reign' (v. 1). The Hebrew verb means something more like 'restrain'. This is not a carte blanche for a dictator.

Even so, the whole experience is a wonderful assurance of God's goodness for Saul. He is given a new heart. As we saw yesterday, sometimes the biggest barrier to God's will can be our own feeling of unworthiness. It's as if we don't believe in God's love for us. But don't we also often doubt God's ability to change people, both ourselves and others? We must have seen in the lives of those around us how love can transform individuals—bringing them truly alive, giving them purpose in their lives—but we associate this transformation most readily with romantic love and finding our true partner. Why can't we see that God does this, too? This isn't just a pattern from the lives of saints and great Christians; it should be happening at our local church, to people we know and to us.

Prayer

Father, give me a new heart, like Saul's, and renew me to become yours today.

RB

1 SAMUEL 10:20–25 (NRSV, ABRIDGED)

Cowering among the baggage

Then Samuel brought all the tribes of Israel [before the Lord]... and Saul the son of Kish was taken by lot. But when they sought him, he could not be found... and the Lord said, 'See, he has hidden himself among the baggage.' Then they ran and brought him from there. When he took his stand among the people, he was head and shoulders taller than any of them. Samuel said to all the people, 'Do you see the one whom the Lord has chosen? There is no one like him among all the people.' And all the people shouted, 'Long live the king!' Samuel told the people the rights and duties of the kingship.

Samuel has anointed Saul in private and now needs to confirm him publicly as ruler over Israel. Part of this process is to draw lots, so that the people can see that God has chosen Saul. When the lot falls on Saul, there is a wonderfully comic scene in which he is hiding. You can imagine the servants searching through the great assembly, desperately trying to find their future leader, who is meant to be the star of the show—and there he is, a big man cowering among the baggage.

When he is brought before the people, they agree that he looks outstanding and acclaim him as king. It's not as simple as that, though, for Samuel reminds everyone that this privilege comes with duties attached. Saul has a new heart and new experience of prophecy, but he is still apprehensive. Even the most confident, gifted people are under the judgment of God. This process of confirming Saul as ruler, and the sense of duty in the process, echo the modern coronation service. In 1953, Queen Elizabeth II was reminded of her place under God and the solemn trust given to her. Some commentators later suggested that her approach to it might be similar to that of a priest being ordained.

This may seem a very long way from our own experience, but each of us has responsibilities—to family, to our community, to our fellow human beings across the world and of course to God. We have to grow up and take all this seriously, not trying to hide.

Prayer

Father, strengthen me to stand tall and carry out your will.

RB

Imitating God's generosity

And the spirit of God came upon Saul in power… and his anger was greatly kindled. He took a yoke of oxen, and cut them in pieces and sent them throughout all the territory of Israel by messengers, saying, 'Whoever does not come out after Saul and Samuel, so shall it be done to his oxen!' Then the dread of the Lord fell upon the people… At the morning watch they came into the camp and cut down the Ammonites until the heat of the day; and those who survived were scattered… The people said to Samuel, 'Who is it that said, "Shall Saul reign over us?" Give them to us so that we may put them to death.' But Saul said, 'No one shall be put to death this day, for today the Lord has brought deliverance to Israel.'

Here we see Saul in action, vindicating the trust placed in him by God and the people. He does well: he credits God with the victory and gives due place to Samuel. This is how it should be.

As we have seen so often, this story makes it sound so simple: the Ammonites threaten the people, who appeal for help; Saul summons an army; the army wins the battle; Saul thanks God for the triumph and the people acclaim Saul. Interwoven with this, though, there are telling details: Saul is possessed by God in righteous anger. He comes up with a dramatic gesture of cutting up oxen, which captures people's imagination (v. 7). Importantly, however, Saul isn't completely ruthless (unless you are an Ammonite…): he refuses to avenge himself on those who doubted his kingship.

All this goes beyond the basic gratitude that we noted last Thursday. It takes the idea further: we thank God for his help and, crucially, become generous in our turn. God is good to us, so then we can be good to others. We can imitate his love in our own way. But do we really do this? We should pause, think a little, and try it. It would mean thanking God for simple things, such as a safe journey or a small act of kindness, and then turning that spark of warm gratitude into a positive act for others.

For reflection

What can I do today to celebrate my thankfulness to God?

RB

1 Samuel 12:1, 14–22 (NRSV, abridged)

'Do not be afraid'

Samuel said to all Israel, 'I have listened to you in all that you have said to me, and have set a king over you... if both you and the king who reigns over you will follow the Lord your God, it will be well; but if you will not heed the voice of the Lord, but rebel against the commandment of the Lord, then the hand of the Lord will be against you and your king.' ... Samuel called upon the Lord, and the Lord sent thunder and rain that day; and all the people greatly feared the Lord and Samuel... And Samuel said to the people, 'Do not be afraid; you have done all this evil, yet do not turn aside from following the Lord... For the Lord will not cast away his people.'

Samuel is addressing all the people. Earlier, he reminded them of what God had done for them, but the heart of his message is here: if you 'follow the Lord your God, it will be well', but if you don't... Samuel then calls down rain and thunder, out of season, as a sign of God's power. This produces the required expression of penitence from the people, which Samuel meets with a gracious response. Movingly, he reassures them: 'Do not be afraid.'

This speech is headed 'Samuel's Farewell Address' in the NRSV. It marks the end of an era. The old time of the prophets ends with Samuel, who would not take bribes. The contrast is implied with the new age of kingship, as Samuel has already warned that the king will require more money in taxes and service from the Israelites' children (8:11–18).

Whatever ill Israel may have done, however, everything can be redeemed by the people's faithfulness to God. They still have a chance to do the right thing. God gives them help in Samuel, who fulfils the traditional prophet's function of intercession and instruction (12:23). God gives us a chance in just the same way—and help from others, too. No matter what we have done, even the most evil person can turn back to God.

For reflection

Is there a sin or sense of unworthiness from your past that stops you trusting God? Do you need to turn from it and move towards him?

RB

The end doesn't justify the means

[Saul] waited for seven days, the time appointed by Samuel; but Samuel did not come to Gilgal, and the people began to slip away from Saul... As soon as he had finished offering the burnt-offering, Samuel arrived... [He] said, 'What have you done?' Saul replied, '... I forced myself, and offered the burnt-offering.' Samuel said to Saul, 'You have done foolishly; you have not kept the commandment of the Lord your God... now your kingdom will not continue; the Lord has sought out a man after his own heart; and the Lord has appointed him to be ruler over his people.'

Saul is fighting the Philistines and knows he needs God's help. He waits the allotted time for Samuel to come and offer sacrifice but, when the prophet doesn't turn up, he decides to go ahead and offer the sacrifice—a privilege that Samuel claimed for himself alone, as prophet. So Samuel arrives and curses Saul.

At first glance, the punishment in Samuel's curses seems disproportionate—the ending of Saul's rule and his replacement by a better man—but Saul should have had his priorities straight. The end does not justify the means. He should have sought the Lord's favour in the correct way and not taken a shortcut. Did he really think he could fool God and still have the blessing? This is just one episode among a number: Saul also goes on to disobey God in chapter 15, twisting God's commands.

We all have our own ways of trying to play this game with God. How often have we slyly bargained with him: 'I mean well—surely it doesn't matter if I bend the rules to get in a better position? I can do so much good later.' It's as if a Christian told a lie to win funding for a charity project (and that's not as unlikely a scenario as you might think). We might think it was OK to misrepresent the truth a little, as we would do worthwhile things with the money in the end. Of course, we can see this more clearly in others' lives, forgetting our own faults.

For reflection

Have I ever pretended to myself that I can fool God? Have I been dishonest, thinking that good might come out of it?

RB

The Lord looketh on the heart

And the Lord said unto Samuel, How long wilt thou mourn for Saul...? Fill thine horn with oil, and go, I will send thee to Jesse the Bethlehemite: for I have provided me a king among his sons... [Samuel] looked on Eliab, and said, Surely the Lord's anointed is before him. But the Lord said unto Samuel, Look not on his countenance, or on the height of his stature; because I have refused him: for the Lord seeth not as man seeth; for man looketh on the outward appearance, but the Lord looketh on the heart.' ... And [Jesse] sent, and brought [David] in. Now he was ruddy, and withal of a beautiful countenance, and goodly to look to. And the Lord said, Arise, anoint him: for this is he.

Samuel can't understand why God rejects the highly presentable elder sons of Jesse. Last time, God chose a tall man in Saul, but now he specifically refuses such a criterion. This time, 'the Lord looks on the heart'.

So how is it that the chosen one, David, is 'handsome'? Doesn't this undermine the denials about outward appearance? There is a clue in the words 'ruddy' and 'with a beautiful countenance'. They imply a liveliness, a spark of vigour that marks a person's character. We all know how attractive individuals can seem because of their bright manner, regardless of conventional beauty. Surely David has that type of charisma—like an actor with a particular presence, you can't take your eyes off him, whether or not he's the best-looking man on the stage.

This combination of character and looks is a gift from God. When you meet some Christians with this combination, you can tell that they know and love God and spend time in prayer. They glow.

Such a hope for the future is a fitting place to leave Samuel, who appears in only one or two more episodes, which say more about those around him than about him. His death is described within a single verse, when all Israel mourned (1 Samuel 25:1). The rest of us might feel that he is like Shakespeare's King Lear, in that 'we that are young / Shall never see so much, nor live so long.'

Prayer

Father, draw me to you, so that I may reflect some small part of your goodness and beauty.

RB

Job 28—42

The first time I read the book of Job, I was lying in bed in a Scottish guesthouse with acute abdominal pain, clutching a hot-water bottle and a bottle of brandy, and wondering if I would need to be airlifted to Skye for an appendectomy. I read Job from end to end (thank goodness for Gideon Bibles) and found it oddly comforting. (I didn't have that appendectomy, by the way; it was just an infection.)

It seems to me that not many Christians read Job these days. If they did read it, they wouldn't be able, as some do, to preach a 'gospel' of prosperity and freedom from suffering for all who follow Jesus. That kind of gospel is one that few of the early Christians would have been able to recognize, persecuted and martyred as so many of them were.

The book of Job is a lengthy, determined attempt to answer those tricky questions encountered by almost anyone who tries to communicate their faith to others. If God is good, why do the innocent suffer? Why do bad things happen to good people? Why does God not protect his own, as he apparently promises to do?

The book belongs with the 'wisdom' writings of the Old Testament, such as Proverbs and Ecclesiastes. These writings offer insights into the challenges of daily living—the 'discipleship books', as it were, of their day. No one knows who wrote Job or when, although it's clearly very ancient, written using the framework of an early belief in a 'council of heavenly beings', who gather before God to get their 'assignments'. 'The Satan' is included in this gathering. It's also written very much in the context of a belief that all suffering is caused by sin, and it sets out to interrogate that belief.

The intriguing thing about the book is that the big question it addresses is never actually answered, at least not in any way that can be put into words. By the end, though, Job doesn't need that sort of answer any more. He has found a bigger answer—or is it a bigger question?

The closing chapters are full of human emotion and of longing for truth. They are also some of the best poetry ever written. Try reading the whole book at one go some time, for a rollercoaster ride of life and faith.

Veronica Zundel

JOB 28:1–4, 12–15 (NRSV)

A mine of information?

Surely there is a mine for silver, and a place for gold to be refined. Iron is taken out of the earth, and copper is smelted from ore. Miners put an end to darkness, and search out to the farthest bound the ore in gloom and deep darkness. They open shafts in a valley away from human habitation; they are forgotten by travellers, they sway suspended, remote from people... But where shall wisdom be found? And where is the place of understanding? Mortals do not know the way to it, and it is not found in the land of the living. The deep says, 'It is not in me', and the sea says, 'It is not with me.' It cannot be bought for gold, and silver cannot be weighed out as its price.

Before university, my husband spent a year working for the then Coal Board down a Welsh mine. Even with modern technology, mining is a dark, dirty, dangerous job and he didn't go back to work for them after his degree!

In Old Testament times, mining must have been a living hell. Yet, for the sake of gold, iron or precious stones, men took the risk (or perhaps got slaves to take it for them). Wisdom, however, Job asserts, is buried deeper even than the rare substances found underground. Picks and shovels can't dig it out and it isn't sold at the market. Job and his friends have sat for long hours, searching in the darkness of their minds for wisdom to address his terrible situation, and still the answers don't bring satisfaction.

What is wisdom, anyway? Later, my husband became a computer consultant. With the rise of 'information technology', if wisdom were built up from information, he and all of us would be very wise (he is, of course, but not from computers)—but wisdom isn't the same as information.

Last night I watched the documentary film *Spellbound*, about the US national spelling bee. Twelve-year-old children managed to spell out the most obscure words—but wisdom isn't learned by rote. Tomorrow we will find out what the writer of Job defines as wisdom.

Prayer

'Even the darkness is not dark to you; the night is as bright as the day, for darkness is as light to you'
(Psalm 139:12).

VZ

The mind of God

Where then does wisdom come from? And where is the place of understanding? It is hidden from the eyes of all living, and concealed from the birds of the air. Abaddon and Death say, 'We have heard a rumour of it with our ears.' God understands the way to it, and he knows its place. For he looks to the ends of the earth, and sees everything under the heavens. When he gave to the wind its weight, and apportioned out the waters by measure; when he made a decree for the rain, and a way for the thunderbolt; then he saw it and declared it; he established it, and searched it out. And he said to humankind, 'Truly, the fear of the Lord, that is wisdom; and to depart from evil is understanding.'

When I asked the members of an internet bulletin board where they found glimpses of God, an overwhelming majority said, 'In the created world.' Something about the prolific growth of nature, the beauty of its details, speaks to us of a spirit, a great imagination, behind it. Where else would you look for knowledge of creators but in their works? I can know all kinds of biographical details about Van Gogh, but I don't really know Van Gogh until I know his paintings.

Scientist Stephen Hawking writes that if we found the elusive 'unified theory of everything', we would know 'the mind of God'. The writer of Job likewise looks for God's wisdom in the mindblowing complexity of the universe.

Yet this writer, in the mouth of Job, is not quite saying, 'God and God's wisdom are found in creation.' After all, like Richard Dawkins, you can be a great scientist and a committed atheist. Rather, God's wisdom is in our response to creation.

Writer Gerard Hughes talks of a false image of God as 'good old Uncle George', whom you are meant to love and visit regularly, but who threatens to throw you into the fire in his basement if you don't. The 'fear' spoken of here is not the fear one might feel of 'Uncle George'. It is awe, wonder, respect—a response that is meant to be expressed in following God's way of love and goodness.

Prayer

Pray Solomon's prayer: 'Give me now wisdom and knowledge'
(2 Chronicles 1:10).

VZ

The milk of human kindness

O that I were as in the months of old, as in the days when God watched over me; when his lamp shone over my head, and by his light I walked through darkness... when the Almighty was still with me, when my children were around me; when my steps were washed with milk, and the rock poured out for me streams of oil! When I went out to the gate of the city, when I took my seat in the square, the young men saw me and withdrew, and the aged rose up and stood... When the ear heard, it commended me, and when the eye saw, it approved; because I delivered the poor who cried, and the orphan who had no helper.

The super-rich, even when they give away lots of money in philanthropy, are not by any means necessarily happy people—with a few notable exceptions. Job is portrayed here as one such exception: a man who, while wealthy, also has a family he can be proud of (rare in rich kids!) and takes a prominent part in economic and judicial life. He gains as much happiness from bringing the poor out of poverty and protecting the vulnerable child as he does from having a splendid house or dozens of camels. (I suppose the modern equivalent would be several vintage cars in the garage!)

It is nowhere suggested that Job has bought his way into his social standing; on the contrary, it is his wisdom, good judgment and generosity that earn him the respect of his fellow 'councillors'. We joke sometimes about public servants, the 'great and the good', defining them as 'worthies', honourable but somewhat dull. In his reminiscences, though, Job gives the impression that he was loved as well as admired.

Job doesn't appear to be trying to justify himself before God by his past endeavours. As the psalmists often do, he is merely expressing his longing for the old days and his lament that they are over. It is a cry to God, honest and vulnerable.

Often we feel, or others teach us, that we ought only to be positive in prayer. Job shows us that we can 'tell it like it is'.

Reflection

Grief and loss are emotions we can safely express to God, and to trusted others. Do you need to lament?

VZ

Mocking the afflicted

But now they make sport of me, those who are younger than I, whose fathers I would have disdained to set with the dogs of my flock... And now they mock me in song; I am a byword to them. They abhor me, they keep aloof from me; they do not hesitate to spit at the sight of me. Because God has loosed my bowstring and humbled me, they have cast off restraint in my presence. On my right hand the rabble rise up; they send me sprawling, and build roads for my ruin. They break up my path, they promote my calamity; no one restrains them... Terrors are turned upon me; my honour is pursued as by the wind, and my prosperity has passed away like a cloud.

In the past couple of years I have been the 'host' for a private internet discussion board for people, mostly Christians, with mental health difficulties. One of the commonest stories I hear is that fellow church members say things like 'Christians don't get depressed' or 'If you had more faith, you could be healed'. I've heard that people with lifelong disabilities often get this treatment too.

Job has been hearing this sort of comment longer than anyone might be expected to bear it. His friends have spent nearly 30 chapters telling him he must have sinned to have suffered so and that if only he repents, everything will go right again.

Perhaps it is a way of expressing his frustration without directly accusing his friends that he now lets off a volley of complaints about the 'rabble' who are making fun of his predicament. It's easier to lay the blame on someone 'out there', people who have no respect or sympathy, rather than face the lack of compassion within the community of faith.

Yet we need to examine ourselves, too. Do we avoid the bereaved because we don't know what to say? Do we secretly enjoy passing on gossip disguised as a request for prayer? Our compassion fatigue may be less blatant and raucous than that of the 'yobs' who mock Job, but it is still less than the best.

Reflection

God never told us to lecture those who weep or try to cheer up those who weep, but to weep with them (see Romans 12:15).

VZ

Pleading innocence

If my step has turned aside from the way, and my heart has followed my eyes, and if any spot has clung to my hands; then let me sow, and another eat; and let what grows for me be rooted out. If my heart has been enticed by a woman, and I have lain in wait at my neighbour's door; then let my wife grind for another, and let other men kneel over her... If I have withheld anything that the poor desired, or have caused the eyes of the widow to fail, or have eaten my morsel alone, and the orphan has not eaten from it... if I have seen anyone perish for lack of clothing, or a poor person without covering... if I have raised my hand against the orphan, because I saw I had supporters at the gate; then let my shoulder blade fall from my shoulder, and let my arm be broken from its socket.

One of the statements of Paul that I find most difficult (and there are many!) is that declaration made in his speech to the Sanhedrin: 'Brothers, up to this day I have lived my life with a clear conscience before God' (Acts 23:1). For myself, I *never* feel my conscience is clear! Motherhood, of course, is a great producer of guilt, and so is depression, which I suffer from.

That's why I'm in awe of Job, who in the midst of desolation can boldly declare his innocence. Unlike some Christians, he does not seem to feel that the only way to God is to accuse oneself of being less than a worm. In spite of all that has happened, he is confident that, as far as it lies in his power, he has lived a righteous life. I've long thought that telling people that they are all gross sinners in order to convince them of the importance of the gospel message is inappropriate and often manipulative. It is not what Jesus, or the apostles, did. Yes, we all fall short of the glory of God, but the good news isn't that we're all doomed, it's that, in spite of all our failings, God inexplicably, extravagantly loves us.

Reflection

If your telling of the gospel doesn't start with 'You are a doomed sinner', what else might it start with?

VZ

God doesn't owe us

Then Elihu son of Barachel the Buzite, of the family of Ram, became angry. He was angry at Job because he justified himself rather than God; he was angry also at Job's three friends because they had found no answer, though they had declared Job to be in the wrong... Elihu continued and said: 'Do you think this to be just? You say, "I am in the right before God." If you ask, "What advantage have I? How am I better off than if I had sinned?" I will answer you and your friends with you. Look at the heavens and see; observe the clouds, which are higher than you. If you have sinned, what do you accomplish against him? And if your transgressions are multiplied, what do you do to him? If you are righteous, what do you give to him; or what does he receive from your hand? Your wickedness affects others like you, and your righteousness, other human beings.'

It's almost a cliché: along comes the young stranger who will rescue the situation. Yet Elihu's suggestions as to why Job has suffered seem to me generally no better than those of the other three and, at the end of the book, God pronounces *Job* to have spoken rightly of him, not Elihu.

For these reasons, I tend to agree with the scholars who believe that this section is a later addition: a last-ditch attempt to prove that bad things really do only happen to bad people.

This doesn't mean we can't learn anything from Elihu. I remember talking to a young man whose marriage had collapsed. 'I don't understand it,' he said. 'I've always obeyed God's rules, yet this has happened.' Elihu, however, reminds us that our acts of goodness, however sacrificial, do not add up merit points on some sort of divine tally.

This doesn't make our good deeds bad, as some seem to believe, but we must never think that, because of them, we are in a privileged position with God. God's love for us is always unearnt.

It is for the sake of other people, Elihu declares, that we do good—and that alone is reason enough to do it.

Reflection

'Why do you call me good? No one is good but God alone'
(Mark 10:18).

VZ

Treasures of darkness

Surely God is mighty and does not despise any; he is mighty in strength of understanding. He does not keep the wicked alive, but gives the afflicted their right... He delivers the afflicted by their affliction, and opens their ear by adversity... But you are obsessed with the case of the wicked; judgment and justice seize you... Will your cry avail to keep you from distress, or will all the force of your strength? Do not long for the night, when peoples are cut off in their place. Beware! Do not turn to iniquity; because of that you have been tried by affliction. See, God is exalted in his power; who is a teacher like him? Who has prescribed for him his way, or who can say, 'You have done wrong'?

The 2006 film *Little Miss Sunshine* is a hilarious comedy, but with a dark seam of reality running through it. In one scene, an uncle and nephew are leaning on a wall overlooking the sea. The nephew is severely depressed, hasn't spoken for months, and has just learnt that his lifetime's ambition is impossible for him to achieve.

The uncle, who has suffered in his own life from unrequited love, tells the boy that one day he will look back and realize that this period of suffering was actually the most significant period of his life and that, without the dark times, none of us can mature into what we're meant to be. It's a very moving scene and reminded me of some dark times in my own life.

So here's another thing that Elihu has got right: while we may not be able to explain why things have gone wrong in our life, we can still learn from them. Indeed, they may be the very thing that God uses to bring us to 'the full stature of Christ' (Ephesians 4:13).

This, of course, is not necessarily just what we want to hear in the midst of our worst times, but we may need to hear the other point that Elihu makes: that becoming 'obsessed with... the wicked', with why good people suffer and bad people seem to thrive, will do us no good at all.

Prayer

Father, give me the 'treasures of darkness and riches hidden in secret places' (see Isaiah 45:3).

VZ

The mystery at the heart

God thunders wondrously with his voice; he does great things that we cannot comprehend. For to the snow he says, 'Fall on the earth'; and the shower of rain, his heavy shower of rain, serves as a sign on everyone's hand, so that all whom he has made may know it. Then the animals go into their lairs and remain in their dens. From its chamber comes the whirlwind, and cold from the scattering winds. By the breath of God ice is given, and the broad waters are frozen fast. He loads the thick cloud with moisture; the clouds scatter his lightning. They turn round and round by his guidance, to accomplish all that he commands them on the face of the habitable world. Whether for correction, or for his land, or for love, he causes it to happen. Hear this, O Job; stop and consider the wondrous works of God.

Many years ago, on a clear cold night, I saw a full rainbow around the moon—not just a bright haze, but a complete, seven-coloured moonbow. It's a once-in-a-lifetime sight that I shall never forget.

For me, it was the sheer beauty that evoked my wonder; for Elihu, it's the drama of thunder, lightning and blizzards. If these, he seems to imply, are beyond our comprehension, how can we expect to understand the course of our own lives?

Nowadays we understand a great deal about storms, snow and even, I presume, moonbows and how they arise. Does this make us less inclined to attribute them to the work of God? For many scientists who are also Christians, knowing how they 'work' only arouses more wonder. I learned yesterday from the radio that the earth's core is as hot as the sun. Isn't it amazing that we can walk on its crust?

In this passage, Elihu foreshadows the 'answer' that God will give to Job at the end of the book. Whatever we may understand about the world, God is the mystery at its heart; and if we want to live with God, we must learn to live with mystery.

Reflection

'But when I thought how to understand this, it seemed to me a wearisome task, until I went into the sanctuary of God; then I perceived their end' (Psalm 73:16–17).

VZ

God gets a word in

Then the Lord answered Job out of the whirlwind: 'Who is this that darkens counsel by words without knowledge? Gird up your loins like a man, I will question you, and you shall declare to me. Where were you when I laid the foundation of the earth? Tell me, if you have understanding. Who determined its measurements—surely you know! ... Or who shut in the sea with doors when it burst out from the womb?—when I made the clouds its garment, and thick darkness its swaddling band, and prescribed bounds for it, and set bars and doors, and said, "Thus far shall you come, and no farther, and here shall your proud waves be stopped"? ... Where is the way to the dwelling of light, and where is the place of darkness, that you may take it to its territory and that you may discern the paths to its home? Surely you know, for you were born then, and the number of your days is great!'

I just had a phone call from a friend who can't understand why God has let her go through family break-up, poverty and illness. It sounds all too familiar... So what answer does God give to all Job's agonized questioning? Certainly he doesn't give any reason why these sufferings have happened. In spite of the prologue, which puts us 'in the know' about Satan's desire to test Job, God doesn't even give him the answer that 'this has happened to test your faith'.

Instead we get what looks like divine sarcasm: 'Of course, Job, you can expect to understand suffering, for after all, you were there when the world was made, weren't you?'

This might seem less than kind!

Is God merely flaunting his power to say 'Look what I can do, so shut up, Job'? I don't think so. I think this is really a gentle encouragement: sometimes, laughter is the best cure for anger. What the writer is saying is that our understanding is very limited—so limited, indeed, that the proper response is to laugh at ourselves for even daring to think we could solve the ancient problem of suffering. We can, however, trust in the power and care of God.

Prayer

Through cloud and sunshine,
O Lord, abide with me.

VZ

Creator and sustainer

'Do you know when the mountain goats give birth? Do you observe the calving of the deer? Can you number the months that they fulfil, and do you know the time when they give birth, when they crouch to give birth to their offspring, and are delivered of their young? Their young ones become strong, they grow up in the open; they go forth, and do not return to them... Is the wild ox willing to serve you? Will it spend the night at your crib? Can you tie it in the furrow with ropes, or will it harrow the valleys after you? Will you depend on it because its strength is great, and will you hand over your labour to it? Do you have faith in it that it will return, and bring your grain to your threshing-floor?'

In America, and recently in the UK as well, battle lines have been drawn between creationist Christians and the education system over whether 'intelligent design' can be taught in schools alongside, or even instead of, evolution.

Yet until fairly recently, the same voices were not heard campaigning for environmental causes or calling for a reduction in our consumption, or alternative energy sources, to combat climate change. It has tended to seem that one set of people is concerned with how God created the world and another completely separate set with how we can help God's world to survive.

There is no such division for the writer of Job. The God who created is also the God who sustains. Job cannot make sure the goats have healthy offspring or harness the wild ox—but, the implication is, God can. If God so sustains the universe, will he not also sustain Job in the midst of all his disasters?

Today we have a great deal more knowledge of and power over creation, and it is our duty to use that knowledge and power for good. God has delegated the care of the planet to us, and we can destroy or save it. In the end, however, we still depend on God's grace for our survival, as Job did. How can we find a balance between care for creation and faith that the outcome is in God's hands?

Prayer

Forgive us, Lord, for the damage we do to your creation. Teach us to care for it better.

VZ

Learning from the beasts

'Look at Behemoth, which I made just as I made you; it eats grass like an ox. Its strength is in its loins, and its power in the muscles of its belly. It makes its tail stiff like a cedar; the sinews of its thighs are knit together. Its bones are tubes of bronze, its limbs like bars of iron. It is the first of the great acts of God—only its Maker can approach it with the sword... Can you draw out Leviathan with a fish-hook, or press down its tongue with a cord? Can you put a rope in its nose, or pierce its jaw with a hook? Will it make many supplications to you? Will it speak soft words to you? Will it make a covenant with you to be taken as your servant for ever? Will you play with it as with a bird, or will you put it on leash for your girls? ... Lay hands on it; think of the battle; you will not do it again!'

Poetry doesn't always need to be easy to understand in order to be enjoyable. No one knows exactly what Behemoth and Leviathan are, although they may be the hippopotamus and the crocodile. It really doesn't matter; this is still some of the most marvellous poetry ever written about the natural world.

What, though, does it have to say to Job in answer to his suffering? At first sight, it might look something like this: 'Even the beasts God has made are many times more powerful than you, so who do you think you are, Job, to challenge the God who made them?' There's a danger here of portraying God as a kind of 'Godfather', who wants to scare Job into submission.

Maybe, however, there is an-other way of looking at it. Perhaps God wants to recall Job to how small and helpless we are in the face of ultimate reality. Humans are the cleverest creatures, but we are still vulnerable and frail. Our lives are in God's hands and we have no right or ability to decide what they will contain.

Reflection

'You do not even know what tomorrow will bring. What is your life? For you are a mist that appears for a little while and then vanishes'
(James 4:14).

VZ

Face to face

Then Job answered the Lord: 'I know that you can do all things, and that no purpose of yours can be thwarted. "Who is this that hides counsel without knowledge?" Therefore I have uttered what I did not understand, things too wonderful for me, which I did not know. "Hear, and I will speak; I will question you, and you declare to me." I had heard of you by the hearing of the ear, but now my eye sees you; therefore I despise myself, and repent in dust and ashes.'

At the end of C.S. Lewis' marvellous retelling of the myth of Psyche, *Till We Have Faces*, the narrator Orual, after many struggles, comes before a strange veiled figure called 'the judge'. She reads out to this figure her 'complaint against the gods'. When she has finished, he asks, 'Are you answered?' and she says, 'Yes'. The complaint, she goes on to comment, is the answer. To have heard herself making it is the answer, because it has revealed to her who she really is and how narrow her vision has been.

This, however, is not the end of the story. She goes on to have a series of visions, ending with an encounter with 'the god' as she understands him. In his eyes she sees herself transformed into beauty. Then she declares, as she lies dying: 'I know now, Lord, why you utter no answer. You are yourself the answer. Before your face questions die away.'

I think Lewis must have been reading the book of Job when he wrote this! In the face of God's reality, Job has nothing more to say—or else what he has to say cannot be put into words.

Late in his life, the great theologian Thomas Aquinas had a spiritual experience that made everything he had written seem 'like straw' to him, and he wrote nothing more. Likewise, philosopher Blaise Pascal, after an encounter with God, wrote: 'Fire. God of Abraham, God of Isaac, God of Jacob, not of philosophers and scholars. Certainty, certainty, heartfelt joy, peace. God of Jesus Christ.' Before the reality of infinite love, it seems that words fail.

Job has an overwhelming experience of God and no longer needs to know why. The encounter is enough.

Prayer

'God, of your goodness, give me yourself' (Julian of Norwich).

VZ

JOB 42:7–9 (NRSV)

Too many answers?

After the Lord had spoken these words to Job, the Lord said to Eliphaz the Temanite: 'My wrath is kindled against you and against your two friends; for you have not spoken of me what is right, as my servant Job has. Now therefore take seven bulls and seven rams, and go to my servant Job, and offer up for yourselves a burnt-offering; and my servant Job shall pray for you, for I will accept his prayer not to deal with you according to your folly; for you have not spoken of me what is right, as my servant Job has done.' So Eliphaz the Temanite and Bildad the Shuhite and Zophar the Naamathite went and did what the Lord had told them; and the Lord accepted Job's prayer.

In the late 1960s and early 1970s, when I was a young Christian, there was a slogan that often appeared on badges, posters or bumper stickers, which read, 'Jesus is the answer'. It was not long, of course, before some wag added the comment, 'What's the question?' Indeed, no answer will be adequate until we have fully heard the question and the pain behind it. Job's three talkative friends have had plenty of answers as to why he had to endure so much suffering. According to them, Job must have committed some secret sin or taken too much pride in his righteousness, or some other misdemeanour. Sadly, many of these answers are still current today—and they are still as inadequate.

Our hero himself has offered no answers at all—just a long, agonized series of unanswerable questions. But what's this? God is affirming Job for saying the right thing about him, and condemning the friends for peddling lies. This can't be! The friends are so full of pious language; surely God must accept their goodwill?

I find this one of the scariest passages in the Bible. It suggests that much of our well-meaning talk, our attempts to justify God to those who are perplexed, is at best misguided and at worst actually untruthful.

It must be a comfort, however, for those who stick with their questions and refuse easy answers. I pray I might be one of them.

Prayer

Lord who is truth, keep me from over-simplified faith and false comfort.

VZ

Restoration

The Lord blessed the latter days of Job more than his beginning; and he had fourteen thousand sheep, six thousand camels, a thousand yoke of oxen, and a thousand donkeys. He also had seven sons and three daughters. He named the first Jemimah, the second Keziah, and the third Keren-happuch. In all the land there were no women so beautiful as Job's daughters; and their father gave them an inheritance along with their brothers. After this Job lived one hundred and forty years, and saw his children, and his children's children, four generations. And Job died, old and full of days.

There's a small hotel in southern Austria where my parents stayed almost every year for many years. Long before, the proprietors had had a house fire in which all four of their children died. I can't begin to imagine such grief.

They were young enough to have more children, but do you think that would have consoled them for the loss of their family? I very much doubt it. My parents, too, lost a son, and no new child would ever replace him.

For that reason I find this 'happy ending' to Job rather glib—especially as the restoration of livestock is mentioned before the restoration of children! What are we supposed to glean from this tidy dénouement?

Perhaps the book of Job, like the Psalms that follow it in our Bibles, could be seen as a sort of 'Bible in miniature'. We start with what appears to be a perfect situation: a wealthy, righteous, happy man. Our journey takes us through tragedy, confusion, questioning and lostness. At times all sense of God's presence disappears. Sometimes there are glimpses of grace, but they are agonizingly short.

Then, at the end, comes a great restoration. Grief is not denied, but it is swallowed up in joy. The Bible itself has the same shape: it does not promise that there will be restoration in each individual's life, but it does prophesy a great reversal at the end of time, when all tears will be dried (Revelation 21:1–5). As someone said, 'The facts are kind.'

Prayer

Lord, when grief is sharp and faith seems lost, teach me to offer hope without glibness and counsel without condemnation; and give all of us trust in your great promise.

VZ

Romans 1—8

Paul's letter to the Christians in Rome is one of the most influential documents in the New Testament and possibly in the history of the Christian faith. It was instrumental in the spiritual awakening of three of the most influential figures in that history—Augustine of Hippo, Martin Luther and John Wesley. Its teaching lies behind much of the Church's formal theology and in many respects it is the most coherent exposition we have of what we might call the Christian 'case'.

It is sad, then, that for many Christians today it is largely a closed book. Apart from a few well-loved verses, it is generally neglected. I notice that when Romans appears in the lectionary, preachers tend to go for the Old Testament alternative, feeling that Romans is rather deep for ordinary mortals. Yet when, a while ago, I preached on Romans for weeks on end to village congregations, people were surprised at how fresh, relevant and, yes, exciting it is.

For the next three weeks we shall be immersed in the first eight chapters of this book. We shall see how Paul expands its central theme—the 'righteousness', faithfulness or justice of God and its relationship to faith—how he explains the principle of 'Jew first, then to the Gentiles', and how the law relates to faith in Jesus as Messiah and Saviour. From this he expounds his message: grace-through-faith.

Paul probably wrote this letter in about AD57, just after the ones to Corinth. His remaining ambition was to carry the gospel to the 'regions beyond', by which he meant Spain. To do that, he felt he needed the financial and prayer backing of the Christians in Rome. They had recently been through a time of turmoil, with the emperor Claudius expelling many Jews from the city as 'troublemakers'. The 'trouble' may well have been caused by tensions between the synagogues and breakaway groups of Jewish and Gentile God-fearers who had come to believe in Jesus.

The wave of expulsions was now over, Claudius was gone, Jews were returning to the city and the growing Christian community was probably eager to hear the sort of explanation of the faith that Paul offered in this letter.

I'm sure they hung on his words as they were read in their house-groups. I hope, as we read and reflect on it today, we may sense afresh how relevant, intellectually brilliant and compelling it still is.

David Winter

Called to be saints

Paul, a servant of Jesus Christ, called to be an apostle, set apart for the gospel of God, which he promised beforehand through his prophets in the holy scriptures, the gospel concerning his Son, who was descended from David according to the flesh and was declared to be Son of God with power according to the spirit of holiness by resurrection from the dead, Jesus Christ our Lord, through whom we have received grace and apostleship to bring about the obedience of faith among all the Gentiles for the sake of his name, including yourselves who are called to belong to Jesus Christ. To all God's beloved in Rome, who are called to be saints: Grace to you and peace from God our Father and the Lord Jesus Christ.

We have to feel sympathy for Paul's secretary, Tertius (16:22), who was trying to write down these words as they tumbled from the apostle's lips. This passage sets the theme for the whole letter, placing it in a trinitarian context (vv. 1, 4), relating it to the life, death and resurrection of Jesus (vv. 3, 4) and explaining both his apostolic authority and the purpose of his ministry: 'to bring about the obedience of faith among the Gentiles'. He also identifies those to whom he is writing: 'all God's beloved in Rome, who are called to be saints'. We might paraphrase that as 'all the Christians in Rome, on the journey to holiness'.

There was a large Jewish presence in the capital. Before the expulsions under Claudius, one estimate puts the figure at 40,000 and, by the time Paul was writing this letter, the number was probably back at that level. Most of the Christians had found Christ through their contact with the synagogues. Jews became convinced that Jesus was the promised Messiah; Gentiles, initially attracted by the monotheism of the Jews, were drawn to Jesus whose gospel was for the whole world. Both believing Jews and Gentile converts were 'called to be saints'—people whose destiny, by the grace of God, was to be 'made holy'.

Reflection

Today, Remembrance Sunday, we remember those who have died in war. They weren't necessarily 'saintly', but, as Jesus said, to give one's life for others is to show the 'greatest love' (John 15:13). Those 'called to be saints' will also be more concerned with 'giving' than 'getting'.

DW

The life of faith

For I am not ashamed of the gospel; it is the power of God for salvation to everyone who has faith, to the Jew first and also to the Greek. For in it the righteousness of God is revealed through faith for faith; as it is written, 'The one who is righteous will live by faith.'

Now Paul moves to the central theme of his letter: what is meant by God's 'righteousness' and how it is now available to those who believe in Christ. 'Righteousness' is a great and crucial word in the Old Testament. When applied to a human being, it meant 'doing what God requires'—in old-fashioned language, being 'godly'. When applied to God, it refers to his righteous *purpose*, which is that his human creatures should be delivered from evil: it's sometimes translated as 'deliverance' (see, for example, Psalm 51:14).

The word may sound almost threatening to us. God is righteous—that is, holy and good—and might be expected to judge us by his own standards. This is what is known as judicial righteousness. But what the Hebrew scriptures constantly assert is God's *saving* righteousness, by which he reckons sinners as 'righteous'.

Now, that 'power of God for salvation' has been focused in the gospel of Christ—the very gospel that Paul preaches and wishes to explain in this letter. Of course he is not ashamed of it. Indeed, he is proud of it, because by it the saving righteousness of God is made available to everyone who puts their trust in him: 'to the Jew first, and also to the Greek'—that is, the Gentiles.

This gospel of deliverance is revealed 'through faith for faith'— a very compressed kind of statement! Does it mean that through faith in Jesus we find faith? That would seem to say the same thing twice. Is it that the blessings of faith are only available through the exercise of faith? In context, perhaps the most likely interpretation is that through God's faithfulness (to us) we receive the gift of faith.

Whatever it means, the repetition of the word 'faith' sets the scene for the following chapters. Faith is the key that unlocks the door of salvation.

Reflection

If God were not faithful, there would be no point in putting our faith in him.

DW

Futile thinking

For the wrath of God is revealed from heaven against all ungodliness and wickedness of those who by their wickedness suppress the truth. For what can be known about God is plain to them, because God has shown it to them. Ever since the creation of the world his eternal power and divine nature, invisible though they are, have been understood and seen through the things he has made. So they are without excuse; for though they knew God, they did not honour him as God or give thanks to him, but they became futile in their thinking, and their senseless minds were darkened.

The 'wrath of God' is seldom a topic for a Sunday sermon or even a midweek house group discussion nowadays. However, the concept is present all through scripture, from Genesis to Revelation, and our reluctance to contemplate it probably owes more to our own problems with the word 'wrath' when applied to a God of love than anything else. God's wrath is not anger or temper, as though the Almighty were stamping his foot at the naughtiness of his human creatures. It is actually the direct consequence of the conflict between a God of holiness and justice on the one hand and corrupt and evil human actions and attitudes on the other. In the old saying, 'God hates the sin, but loves the sinner'.

We may notice that here and elsewhere in Romans, the condemnation is not of ignorance of God's law, but of a deliberate and wilful decision to reject it. Those under God's wrath 'knew God' but, although they knew him, they still chose another path, becoming 'futile in their thinking', irrational and disobedient. We shall find this emphasis on the need for right thinking elsewhere in the letter (see, for example, 12:2–3), but here Paul is concerned to demonstrate that wilful distortion of truth leads to the distortion of moral values and behaviour and, in the end, to spiritual death. To say that 'God is love' means that he is loving but also that he must hate evil, injustice and exploitation. He hates to see his creation distorted or abused. He loves his creation, and us, too much to tolerate that.

Reflection

Right thinking leads to right attitudes; right attitudes lead to right behaviour. As the saying goes, 'What you think, you are.'

DW

Given up by God

Therefore God gave them up in the lusts of their hearts to impurity, to the degrading of their bodies among themselves, because they exchanged the truth about God for a lie and worshipped and served the creature rather than the Creator, who is blessed for ever! Amen. For this reason God gave them up to degrading passions... And since they did not see fit to acknowledge God, God gave them up to a debased mind and to things that should not be done... They know God's decree, that those who practice such things deserve to die— yet they not only do them but even applaud others who practise them.

This whole passage (and you ought really to read it in full, provided you can take the gory details!) is concerned with the consequences of the 'futile thinking' that Paul was talking about in yesterday's passage. The people under condemnation are those who have effected an exchange (vv. 23, 25, 26)—a deliberate one, in which they have rejected God's truth and glory for a lie. They knew what was right but they chose to do what was wrong. Their fundamental sin was wrong worship, strangely enough—worshipping the 'creature' rather than the Creator.

You don't have to build a physical idol to offer false worship! Idolatry takes many forms, and the apostle sets out some of its manifestations here: sexual depravity (because that is idolatrous worship of physical gratification), covetousness, malice, envy, murder, strife, deceit, craftiness, gossip, pride (vv. 26–31). It's interesting that present-day readers have concentrated on the sexual deeds, which are mostly to do with homosexual behaviour of various kinds. Yet 'gossip'—a prevalent sin in many churches, it has to be said—is in exactly the same list, as are envy, slander and insolence. We can't pick and choose: all sin is rebellion against God and all sin is in one sense idolatry, because it puts human choice in place of the will of God. The great idolatry is the notion that we know better than God.

Reflection

The good news comes later. Sometimes we can't really appreciate it until we have fully absorbed the nature and extent of the bad news.

DW

The 'doers' of the law

All who have sinned apart from the law will also perish apart from the law, and all who have sinned under the law will be judged by the law. For it is not the hearers of the law who are righteous in God's sight, but the doers of the law who will be justified. When Gentiles, who do not possess the law, do instinctively what the law requires, these, though not having the law, are a law to themselves. They show that what the law requires is written on their hearts, to which their own conscience also bears witness; and their conflicting thoughts will accuse or perhaps excuse them on the day when, according to my gospel, God, through Jesus Christ, will judge the secret thoughts of all.

This part of Paul's letter addresses a specific question at a specific point in time, yet it conveys a general truth for all time, and one that is very relevant in our present-day world. He is addressing this problem: has God chosen just one nation for blessing by giving them the law? Does this mean that because only the people of Israel 'hear' the law, only they can be justified?

Not at all, he argues. It is not a matter of hearing the law, even in the Jewish sense of 'attending' to it, but doing what it requires, that makes the difference. Then—probably to the great surprise of his Jewish hearers—he suggests that even Gentiles might, by following their enlightened consciences, actually do what the law requires and so be 'excused' by Jesus Christ on the day of judgment. There's no

hint here that he is referring to Gentile converts to Judaism, either. These are simply 'the people without the law', but he can't rule out the possibility, putting the case no higher than that, that some might truly fear God, be guided by conscience and become 'a law to themselves'. This phrase doesn't mean, as English idiom usually assumes, that they 'do what they like'. Rather, by following their consciences, they do what God likes. Hence, at the judgment, the Saviour of the world will accept them.

Reflection

Here is a warning that our assumptions about who's 'in' and who's 'out' may not tally with God's way of seeing things.

DW

The inwardness of true religion

For a person is not a Jew who is one outwardly, nor is true circumcision something external and physical. Rather, a person is a Jew who is one inwardly, and real circumcision is a matter of the heart—it is spiritual and not literal. Such a person receives praise not from others but from God.

This is a short reading, because it summarizes in succinct language quite a long and tortuous argument, but you will need to read the whole of chapter 2 to appreciate how devastating Paul's words would have been to his more orthodox Jewish hearers. The point he is making is that, while the Jewish people were enormously privileged, because to them God had given the law and the sign of circumcision as a reminder that life itself is his gift, they were not immune to his judgment.

It is as though Paul is engaged in a dialogue with a strict Jew (perhaps the sort of man he was before his conversion—a 'Pharisee of Pharisees'). The opponent puts forward all the evidence of God's particular favour to Israel, and each time Paul turns the argument inside out and shows that God's favour implies responsibility. They simply can't hide behind nationality, race or religion.

That brings him to this final summary—a challenge to all who make a religious profession. How real is it? Circumcision is an out-ward sign, which is meaningless if it is not matched by an inward change. You don't make someone a Jew simply by circumcising them. True circumcision is of the heart, not the male body. (This was not an entirely novel idea: it can be found in Deuteronomy 10:16.)

Circumcision symbolized the indebtedness of humanity to God for life and all its gifts. The act also embraced the whole of Israel, male and female, because of the belief that all life came from this 'seed'. Yet it did not automatically confer the inward change of heart that God requires.

This principle extends beyond Judaism, and Paul's linking of it to baptism (see Colossians 2:21–22) carries a warning for Christians. We might paraphrase, 'A person is not a Christian who is one outwardly (that is, has been baptized), but one whose heart has been baptized.'

Reflection
The evidence, as Paul argues here, is in the life, not the outward show.

DW

Grace as a gift

But now, irrespective of law, the righteousness of God has been disclosed, and is attested by the law and the prophets, the righteousness of God through faith in Jesus Christ for all who believe. For there is no distinction, since all have sinned and fall short of the glory of God; they are now justified by his grace as a gift, through the redemption that is in Christ Jesus, whom God put forward as a sacrifice of atonement by his blood, effective through faith.

'But now'—and the emphasis is on the word 'now'. The story of God's dealings with humanity is at a turning point. Up to 'now', the Jews had the law and the Gentiles had—well, nothing. But in this new era, the righteousness of God, formerly revealed in his law and received by those who kept it truly, is available to 'all who believe'. In what or whom do they believe? 'In Jesus Christ', or Jesus Messiah, as Jews using Hebrew would have understood the phrase.

Wonderfully, this new revelation removes the old distinctions. Negatively, it means that all, whether Jews or Gentiles, who 'sin and fall short of the glory of God' are condemned. Positively, it means that all, whether Jews or Gentiles, who believe in Jesus are 'redeemed'. This is the language of the slave market, an idea that Paul returns to later: those who sin are slaves of sin, but Jesus, by his act of atonement, has won freedom for those who believe.

Buried in these sentences are a couple of words and phrases that are familiar parts of Paul's teaching. One of them is 'grace', amplified here by the words 'as a gift'. That is what grace is—something that we can't earn or deserve but that God gives us. The second is 'in Christ Jesus', which can carry various meanings. Here it means the benefits that are part of what comes to those who put their trust in him. 'In Christ Jesus' there is redemption, freedom, and it can only be received as a gift.

Reflection

Not the labour of my hands
can fulfil thy law's demands;
Could my zeal no respite know,
could my tears for ever flow,
All for sin could not atone;
Thou must save, and Thou alone.

Augustus Toplady (1740–78)
DW

ROMANS 4:16–18 (NRSV)

It all depends on faith

For this reason it depends on faith, in order that the promise may rest on grace and be guaranteed to all his descendants, not only to the adherents of the law but also to those who share the faith of Abraham (for he is the father of all of us, as it is written, 'I have made you the father of many nations')—in the presence of the God in whom he believed, who gives life to the dead and calls into existence the things that do not exist. Hoping against hope, he believed that he would become 'the father of many nations', according to what was said, 'So numerous shall your descendants be.'

This passage comes towards the end of a long argument about the place of Abraham in our justification. Paul could not avoid the topic, because for his Jewish readers Abraham was absolutely central to their understanding of Judaism, and for the Gentiles he was, in one sense, a bit of a problem. For the Jews, he was their 'father', the ancestral head of the whole family of God's people down the ages. For the Gentile believers, Abraham's role as 'father of Israel' might be seen as excluding them from the ranks of God's people.

Paul's argument answers both assumptions. To the Jews, he is at pains to prove that it was Abraham's faith that justified him: he believed God (even when the divine promise seemed impossible of fulfilment) and 'faith was reckoned to him as righteousness' (see v. 9). This faith of Abraham preceded his circumcision—a crucial distinction for Paul.

To the Gentiles, Paul is at pains to stress that part of God's promise to Abraham was that he would be 'the father of many nations', not just Israel. 'For this reason', as this passage begins, 'it depends on faith'—Abraham's faith in God's promises and the believer's faith in the Creator God, who 'gives life to the dead', who makes and keeps his promises. At the end of his argument, Paul pulls the big rabbit out of the hat: that same God 'raised Jesus our Lord from the dead... for our justification' (vv. 24–25).

Reflection

The word 'promise' dominates this whole chapter (vv. 13, 14, 16). We have a God who makes and keeps his promises. That is our hope and the ground of our faith.

DW

Justified by faith

Therefore, since we are justified by faith, we have peace with God through our Lord Jesus Christ, through whom we have obtained access to this grace in which we stand; and we boast in our hope of sharing the glory of God. And not only that, but we also boast in our sufferings, knowing that suffering produces endurance, and endurance produces character, and character produces hope, and hope does not disappoint us, because God's love has been poured into our hearts through the Holy Spirit that has been given to us.

This passage is a kind of bridge between the argument for the priority of faith in justification and the next stage of Paul's exposition, which is the nature of 'grace'. He has touched on it before, but he is now ready to relate it to the saving work of Jesus through his death and resurrection.

Paul begins with a bold statement: 'since we are justified by faith'. This is doubly bold, because he uses the past passive tense: 'having been justified'. Until now, we have been led to think of 'justification' as something in the future, when God's glory is revealed. Without contradicting that idea, Paul wants to stress that the act of faith made by new Christians has had a decisive and eternal effect. They are justified, right now. This has consequences for their way of life, which he will spell out later, but the change has happened.

Because the phrase 'justification by faith' has become something of a party slogan in Christian history, it's important to understand what Paul meant by it. It is a metaphor from the law courts. To justify is to acquit, to say that the person involved is 'righteous'—which is the root of the word in both Hebrew and Greek. Paul will explain very soon how 'sinners' can be declared 'righteous'. Here he contents himself with the single phrase 'through our Lord Jesus Christ' to explain how we can have 'access' to 'this grace in which we stand'. Both the gateway to the king's presence and the curtain to the priestly Holy Place are now open to those who believe in Jesus.

Reflection

There are additional blessings of justification. We have 'peace with God'—shalom, a state of well-being—and we have 'hope', a hope based on God's love poured into our hearts by the Holy Spirit.

DW

ROMANS 5:6–10 (NRSV)

Christ died for sinners

For while we were still weak, at the right time Christ died for the ungodly. Indeed, rarely will anyone die for a righteous person—though perhaps for a good person someone might actually dare to die. But God proves his love for us in that while we still were sinners Christ died for us. Much more surely then, now that we have been justified by his blood, will we be saved through him from the wrath of God. For if while we were enemies, we were reconciled to God through the death of his Son, much more surely, having been reconciled, will we be saved by his life.

Paul turns to one of the great themes of this letter, which is the nature and extent of God's love. He uses a literary .device that seems to have been one of his favourites: comparison. The key phrase is 'much more': if it requires great love to die for a good person, how much more love would it take to die for a bad one? That, says Paul, is what the love of God in Christ is like. While we were still sinners—indeed, 'enemies' (v. 10)—Christ died for us.

The language is of repairing a broken relationship. God was not our enemy, but by disobeying his just and gentle law we have become his enemies. By living sometimes as though he didn't exist, we have become opponents of his purposes. Yet through 'the death of his Son' we have been reconciled to God; the divine–human relationship has been restored.

Having been reconciled through Jesus' death, we will be saved by his risen life. This salvation is the ultimate goal of God's love, brought to completion only when we stand before him in the sinless environment of heaven. We are saved now, in order to be fully saved then.

Note how, in one short passage, we have both the wrath of God and the love of God. Clearly Paul feels no contradiction in speaking of them in the same breath. The wrath of God is a sign of his absolute purity and holiness; he cannot tolerate evil in his good creation. The love of God is also a sign of the pure and holy love that he feels for his creatures.

Reflection

God loves us—not because we are lovable, but because he is love.

DW

Newness of life

What then are we to say? Should we continue in sin in order that grace may abound? By no means! How can we who died to sin go on living in it? Do you not know that all of us who have been baptized into Christ Jesus were baptized into his death? Therefore we have been buried with him by baptism into death, so that, just as Christ was raised from the dead by the glory of the Father, so we too might walk in newness of life. For if we have been united with him in a death like his, we will certainly be united with him in a resurrection like his.

Paul has just been going on about the wonders of grace—the gift of God by which sin is overcome and defeated. But then he realizes how some people might take that idea. If sin provokes God's grace, then surely the more we sin the more grace will abound?

He dismisses this argument in a terse phrase, just two words in Greek: 'By no means!' That would distort the sacrifice of Christ. In baptism, the believer shares in his death: the imagery is of immersion, being 'buried' under the water. We 'die with Christ' to sin— and then we rise with him into 'newness of life'.

Paul puts a rhetorical question: 'How can we who died to sin go on living in it?' He doesn't mean 'How can a Christian ever sin?' Sin, sadly, is part of the inevitable experience of a fallen human race. Sinless perfection is not part of the deal, but freedom from the domi-

nation of sin certainly is. To 'go on living in it'—the tense is present continuous—would be inconsistent with the life of grace.

Some words from the first letter of John provide an appropriate commentary on Paul's words here. 'I am writing these things to you so that you may not sin' (there's the principle: Christians don't live a life of sin). 'But if anyone sins…' (there's the experience of the Christian: sometimes we fail) 'we have an advocate with the Father, Jesus Christ the righteous; and he is the atoning sacrifice for our sins' (1 John 2:1–2).

Reflection

To walk 'in newness of life'—that is the destiny of the Christian who by grace shares the risen life of Christ.

DW

A new dominion

But if we have died with Christ, we believe that we will also live with him. We know that Christ, being raised from the dead, will never die again; death no longer has dominion over him. The death he died, he died to sin, once for all; but the life he lives, he lives to God. So you also must consider yourselves dead to sin and alive to God in Christ Jesus. Therefore, do not let sin exercise dominion in your mortal bodies, to make you obey their passions. No longer present your members to sin as instruments of wickedness, but present yourselves to God as those who have been brought from death to life, and present your members to God as instruments of right-eousness. For sin will have no dominion over you, since you are not under law but under grace.

This passage continues Paul's explanation of the link between the death and resurrection of Jesus and the life of the believer. The Christian has been 'buried with Christ by baptism' (v. 4). Jesus died for sin—so that it could be forgiven. The believer is so closely united to him that he or she also 'dies' with him, not in this case for sin, but to sin. Because Christ has died for sin, sin is dead, not in the sense that it has ceased to exist but that it has lost its power. That means in practice for the believers that sin (and therefore spiritual death) no longer has any power over them. They are to reckon themselves dead to sin and alive to God in Christ Jesus.

This is admittedly a very complicated line of argument, but Paul wanted to emphasize that believers are new people in Christ, free from the stranglehold of sin. This is an essential part of his answer to the rhetorical question at the start of this chapter, 'Should we continue in sin?' The answer is simple: of course we shouldn't, because the death of Jesus for sin has freed us from its 'dominion'.

Reflection

Do we consider ourselves under the rule and dominion of the very sin for which Christ died? Or are we under the rule and dominion of the God who raised Jesus from the dead? These are questions that Paul will return to later, but they face us every day of our lives.

DW

The two slaveries

What then? Should we sin because we are not under law but under grace? By no means! Do you not know that if you present yourselves to anyone as obedient slaves, you are slaves of the one whom you obey, either of sin, which leads to death, or of obedience, which leads to righteousness? But thanks be to God that you, having once been slaves of sin, have become obedient from the heart to the form of teaching to which you were entrusted, and that you, having been set free from sin, have become slaves of righteousness. I am speaking in human terms because of your natural limitations. For just as you once presented your members as slaves to impurity and to greater and greater iniquity, so now present your members as slaves to righteousness for sanctification.

Now Paul expands the idea of 'dominion'. He suggests that we are all slaves: we are owned and controlled either by sin or by righteousness. The apostle wanted the believers in Rome to understand the choice before them. Would they live as their neighbours did or would they carve out a truly Christian lifestyle, utterly distinct from that of their contemporaries? The language he chooses is stark. For him, it is one or the other.

There are, he says, two slaveries. The first is to sin, 'which leads to death'. The second is to righteousness, which leads to life. As we have seen earlier, 'righteousness' is a key word in this letter, and is regarded by Paul as virtually synonymous with God, the truly righteous one. To become slaves to sin, we simply follow our fallen instincts. To become 'slaves' of God, we need to learn obedience, to offer ourselves to the Righteous One and to step on to the path that leads to holiness. All of this is made possible by obeying from the heart 'the form of teaching to which you were entrusted' (v. 17). Presumably this is a reference to their pre-baptism instruction in the gospel. Paul offers thanks to God that they have done this and stepped from the ugly bondage of evil into the glorious freedom of the servants of God.

Reflection

Christians are 'not under the law but under grace'. This does not mean that they are free to sin, but that they are free to live as God's children in God's world.

DW

Who will rescue me?

So I find it to be a law that when I want to do what is good, evil lies close at hand. For I delight in the law of God in my inmost self, but I see in my members another law at war with the law of my mind, making me captive to the law of sin that dwells in my members. Wretched man that I am! Who will rescue me from this body of death? Thanks be to God through Jesus Christ our Lord! So then, with my mind I am a slave to the law of God, but with my flesh I am a slave to the law of sin.

This part of Paul's letter has been argued over for centuries. Is he speaking about himself now, as a mature Christian, or of himself before his conversion? A literal reading suggests the former, but that has been a problem for those who find it hard to believe that the great missionary was also aware of the constant presence in his life not only of temptation, but also of failure. While he knew what he ought to do, and even what he wanted to do, that ever-present shadow of sin would not give in. At times his mind and body felt like a battlefield with good and evil locked in deadly combat.

The reason that most modern commentators favour this interpretation of the passage is that Paul's language so powerfully captures the experience of every Christian. We have not achieved sinless perfection. We are not immune to temptation.

Finally Paul cries out, 'Who will rescue me from this body of death?' The answer, for which he thanks God, is brief and simple: 'the Lord Jesus Christ'. The 'body of death' simply means mortality. Paul didn't think that the body is itself evil. How could it be if Jesus was born and lived as a human? But part of being human, even for Jesus, is the presence of temptation, and for ordinary mortals that means disappointing failure. Yet that same Jesus has conquered both sin and death—and did it in a human body!

Reflection

If we feel like crying out with Paul, 'Who will rescue me from this body of death?' then we can also shout with him, 'Thanks be to God through our Jesus Christ our Lord!'

DW

No condemnation

There is therefore now no condemnation for those who are in Christ Jesus. For the law of the Spirit of life in Christ Jesus has set you free from the law of sin and of death. For God has done what the law, weakened by the flesh, could not do: by sending his own Son in the likeness of sinful flesh, and to deal with sin, he condemned sin in the flesh, so that the just requirement of the law might be fulfilled in us, who walk not according to the flesh but according to the Spirit. For those who live according to the flesh set their minds on the things of the flesh, but those who live according to the Spirit set their minds on the things of the Spirit. To set the mind on the flesh is death, but to set the mind on the Spirit is life and peace.

At the start of the letter, Paul argued that the problem for the 'ungodly' was that their thinking was 'futile' (see 1:18–21). Now we have the positive side of the argument. Just as futile thinking leads to evil and death, so setting our minds on the 'things of the Spirit' brings life and peace.

For his Christian audience, the change has already taken place. They are now under a new law, not one that constantly condemns them for their failure to keep it, but the 'law of the Spirit of life in Christ Jesus', which sets them free from that bondage to failure.

This again shows two ways of living. One is a constant struggle in which human beings fail, so that God's righteous law becomes an instrument of condemnation. But, says Paul, 'there is therefore now no condemnation for those who are in Christ Jesus'. The law of the Spirit of life has set them free from the law of sin and death. This is not to say that the law of God is negative or destructive, but what Paul calls 'the just requirements of the law'—doing what God requires—can only be fulfilled in those who set their minds on the Spirit's goals, who live by the Spirit's promptings.

Reflection

'I will put my law within them, and I will write it on their hearts; and I will be their God, and they shall be my people' (Jeremiah 31:33).

DW

Life-giving Spirit

For this reason the mind that is set on the flesh is hostile to God; it does not submit to God's law—indeed it cannot, and those who are in the flesh cannot please God. But you are not in the flesh; you are in the Spirit, since the Spirit of God dwells in you. Anyone who does not have the Spirit of Christ does not belong to him. But if Christ is in you, though the body is dead because of sin, the Spirit is life because of righteousness. If the Spirit of him who raised Jesus from the dead dwells in you, he who raised Christ from the dead will give life to your mortal bodies also through his Spirit that dwells in you.

Paul continues the theme of flesh–spirit, sometimes implying that the spirit is uppermost, sometimes emphasizing the continuing influence of our mortal nature. If those who are 'in the flesh' cannot please God, but only those who are 'in the Spirit', what does he mean by saying that the Christians in Rome live in bodies that are 'dead because of sin'? Can they not please God?

Throughout Romans we need to keep the same balance in mind. Our bodies are part of the problem, because they are susceptible to sin's enticing power, but the presence of the Spirit in our lives is the answer to the problem. There is now a moral struggle going on in the believer, in contrast to lives where the absence of God's Spirit means that the fallen nature can have free reign. We shouldn't despair when we feel ourselves to be a kind of spiritual battlefield. That's a sign of life, not death!

The difference is the Spirit of God. It is the coming into a person's life of the Holy Spirit that makes a Christian—not baptism, not even faith, but the presence of the very life of God. So 'anyone who does not have the Spirit of Christ does not belong to him'. But if the Spirit is in you, 'though the body is dead because of sin, the Spirit is life because of righteousness'.

Reflection

The body is a precious gift of God, glorified by God in the incarnation—but it is under sentence of death. That's what it means to be 'mortal'. Only the Spirit of God can give life to our dying bodies.

DW

Led by the Spirit of God

So then, brothers and sisters, we are debtors, not to the flesh, to live according to the flesh—for if you live according to the flesh, you will die; but if by the Spirit you put to death the deeds of the body, you will live. For all who are led by the Spirit of God are children of God. For you did not receive a spirit of slavery to fall back into fear, but you have received a spirit of adoption. When we cry, 'Abba! Father!' it is that very Spirit bearing witness with our spirit that we are children of God, and if children, then heirs, heirs of God and joint heirs with Christ—if, in fact, we suffer with him so that we may also be glorified with him.

At last Paul moves into an almost triumphalist mood. Assuming that his hearers in Rome believe and have received the Holy Spirit, the mark of the inward reality of their baptism, then wonderful things follow. Here he sets them out, like trophies on a shelf. Look what is yours in Christ!

First of all, you will live—be fully alive. Then you will be God's children, led by him. (The picture is a touching one—like sheep led by a shepherd, or a group of children led by a parent along safe paths.) As God's children we have the privilege of calling him by his most intimate name, 'Abba'; and as his children, we have absolute title to the inheritance of his names.

Paul puts in a reminder here of conditions attached to these. To be in Christ means are his sufferings (Paul was probably thinking of the persecution that was a constant threat hanging over the church in Rome) as well as the glory that he already enjoys and we shall one day share.

When we pray to God as our Father, that very action is the work of the Spirit of God within us. By the intimacy of our relationship with the Father he is 'bearing witness'—offering evidence to us—that we truly are the children of God.

Reflection

We may sometimes doubt it, especially in times of failure, but our cry for help is all the proof we need that the one who hears our cry is Abba, 'our Father'.

DW

The creation liberated

For the creation waits with eager longing for the revealing of the children of God; for the creation was subjected to futility, not of its own will but by the will of the one who subjected it, in hope that the creation itself will be set free from its bondage to decay and will obtain the freedom of the glory of the children of God. We know that the whole creation has been groaning in labour pains until now; and not only the creation, but we ourselves, who have the first fruits of the Spirit, groan inwardly while we wait for adoption, the redemption of our bodies.

Here is a powerful reminder that when Paul spoke of 'redemption', he had in mind a vaster and more glorious concept than individual salvation. It is, of course, wonderful beyond words that God through Christ has forgiven and justified us, as individuals, and as part of his new people, the Church. But what about the rest of creation? If God loves, values and cherishes everything he has made, then it can scarcely be possible that everything of it except individual human beings is consigned to decay and death.

It's a staggering thought, but Paul's language is unequivocal. The whole creation is waiting, eager for its redemption—its liberation from the effects of death, decay and corruption. God has a plan for the creation that is as comprehensive as his plan for the human race. We and the creation are united both in our 'bondage to decay' and in our longing for liberation from it. Human liberation comes first, apparently—and the creation will enjoy its spectacle, seeing it as a sign of its own eventual redemption. Then, in God's good time, will come the liberation of all things, so that the whole created order will be as he had originally planned it should be.

For this we wait, like a woman awaiting the birth of a child. There will be pain—it's a comparison Jesus once made, too (John 16:21) —but out of the pain there will be joy. As Roman Catholics say at mass each Sunday, we 'wait in joyful hope'.

Reflection
We are redeemed. Our future is secure in Christ, but we still have to await the final masterstroke of our Creator, 'the redemption of our bodies'.

DW

At work for good

We know that all things work together for good for those who love God, who are called according to his purpose. For those whom he foreknew he also predestined to be conformed to the image of his Son, in order that he might be the firstborn within a large family. And those whom he predestined he also called; and those whom he called he also justified; and those whom he justified he also glorified.

This passage includes a well-known statement of confidence in God's providence and a rather less popular exposition of the doctrine of predestination.

The first statement is deeply reassuring. It doesn't say that everything that happens to a Christian is 'good' (in the sense of 'nice' or 'pleasing'). It does say that God is 'at work' in everything that happens in order to bring good out of it. We can see that truth most clearly in the crucifixion of Jesus, but it can be found in many life experiences. Often we find that things we couldn't possibly describe as 'nice' or 'pleasing' (illness, for instance, or even bereavement) can turn into times of profound blessing.

The second statement doesn't say, as some people seem to assume, that God has decided in advance who will be saved and that the rest are therefore doomed. What kind of justice would that be? It does emphasize, however, that the whole process of salvation is an initiative of God. He knows what his 'large family' will be like; he calls us into it; as we respond to his call he justifies us—declares us innocent—and those whom he justifies will eventually share his glory. The apostle is simply asserting a truth already evident in this letter—that our salvation is the work of God from start to finish. All we bring to it is the sin from which we wish to be redeemed.

The two statements are not contradictory. Not only our salvation but also the details of our lives are in the hands of God. This is a long way from fatalism. 'Things' happen in all of our lives, unpredictable things, but because it is God's world and we are his children in it, we are never beyond his endless care.

Reflection

If God is ceaselessly working for our good, should we be looking for signs of his hand at work in our lives?

DW

More than conquerors

Who will separate us from the love of Christ? Will hardship, or distress, or persecution, or famine, or nakedness, or peril, or sword? As it is written, 'For your sake we are being killed all day long; we are accounted as sheep to be slaughtered.' No, in all these things we are more than conquerors through him who loved us.

Paul brings this first half of his letter to a resounding climax. If God has justified those who put their faith in Jesus, if sins are forgiven and the life of the Holy Spirit dwells in the believer, then we are truly free men and women. Who has the right to condemn us? No one, because the only person in a position to do so—Jesus Christ, the one through whom God will judge the world—has died for our forgiveness. More than that, in his risen life he is 'at the right hand of God' interceding for us. His presence before the Father is a guarantee of an unbreakable redemption.

Paul now spells out what that might mean in practice for the Roman Christians. Doubtless they will face hardship in the future. The quotation from Psalm 44:22 takes his readers back to the experience of God's people of old, who also felt that for his sake they were being marked out for opposition and suffering. Now, in the first century, persecution would be a constant threat for Christian citizens of the capital of the empire.

Can any of these things separate them from the love of Christ?

Paul's answer is a simple but resounding 'No'. Of course they can't, because the love of Christ is unconditional. It doesn't depend on our courage or fortitude or ability to face up to persecution. He loved us—'while we were still sinners', as he pointed out earlier (5:8). Is it surprising, then, that he loves us now, as his believing children, baptized into his body? We are not just survivors, either, but 'conquerors'. The love of God in Christ turns defeat into victory.

Reflection

'More than conquerors' sounds like arrogance! Yet Paul's point was that the Christians to whom he was writing would not be bare survivors in the face of all the calamities he had listed, but conquerors. They would triumph over their troubles, confident in the love of Christ.

DW

The love that will not let me go

For I am convinced that neither death, nor life, nor angels, nor rulers, nor things present, nor things to come, nor powers, nor height, nor depth, nor anything else in all creation, will be able to separate us from the love of God in Christ Jesus our Lord.

Paul doesn't often rise to such poetic heights! But the concluding sentences of the first half of this letter show that when he was moved to it (as in 1 Corinthians 13, for instance) he could achieve a magnificence of expression to match the force and power of his intellect.

These words bring the exposition of salvation by grace-through-faith to a conclusion. Paul wanted his hearers to be in no possible doubt about the assurance of their standing in Christ. The bond was absolute, permanent, eternal. Nothing—*nothing*—could separate them from the Saviour. The list of possible barriers is all-inclusive. There is, of course, death, mortality, the final enemy, defeated by the risen Christ. But there is also 'life'—presumably its burdens, problems and afflictions. The events of life cannot separate us from Christ. Neither can 'angels' (that is, spiritual powers), nor earthly rulers like Caesar. Neither can present troubles nor anything that might lie menacingly in the future. Neither can what is high above us or deep below us; and just in case that leaves any threat to this glorious relationship unnamed, he sums it up in a comprehensive phrase: 'nothing else in all creation'.

What is it from which the believer can never be separated? Why, 'the love of God in Christ Jesus our Lord'. All that has gone before is summed up in that one phrase. In Christ, the love of God for his fallen and sinful children has overflowed into the offer of grace-through-faith. Called, justified, glorified, the new people of God can stand utterly secure.

Reflection

It's not surprising that these words are often read at funeral services, sometimes as the coffin is being carried into church. At the very moment when the mourners may feel the pang of separation, these ringing words remind us that ultimately for the believer there is no separation at all. The one who has died and the people in the pews can equally know the assurance of the continuous and unbreakable presence of the love of God in Christ.

DW

Messiah: Jesus in Matthew's Gospel

All four Gospels are thick with links to the Old Testament. Themes and texts from the Hebrew scriptures light up the New Testament message and help to show its meaning. Of the four, it is Matthew who makes this connection most obvious. The Old Testament was his Bible and many of his first readers would have known it well, too. In his Gospel, Matthew showed some of the threads that joined past to present, and connected Israel's heritage and scripture to the good news of Jesus.

The Gospel writers were pastors, writing to help people grow in the Christian life. The ways they told the Jesus story were shaped by their personal experience and also by the people and communities among whom they lived. Matthew's Gospel feels very Jewish in its style and in its constant attention to the Old Testament. He was writing, surely, with Jewish people particularly in mind.

This was Matthew's own background and he had found in Jesus the fulfilment of his people's ancient faith. He believed that Jesus was Israel's promised Messiah and he wanted his readers to believe this too. God had not rubbed out their heritage, but had brought them into a glad new era. The Messiah had come. There were new reasons to trust, and fresh meaning in the old story.

In the days ahead we trace some of the ways in which Matthew writes about Jesus. Again and again we shall hear echoes of the Old Testament, resonating with the notes of the Gospel story. As Advent starts today, it is good to look back in faith, for God's purposes run through the years. Time is his territory.

Yet most of the Christians who read the Gospel today are not Jewish. We do not start where many of Matthew's readers had started: they knew the Old Testament and needed help to see it fulfilled in the Gospel. We know the Gospel, but we sometimes forget where it comes from. Matthew's Gospel is a reminder that the Church's faith comes out of Israel. Our faith is Jewish in its roots and now worldwide in its spread. Matthew's Gospel reminds us of these roots and helps us to listen to the melody of the Gospel with the rhythms of Old Testament belief running beneath. In the whole music of scripture, we hear the voice of God. Jesus is Messiah, the hub of the Bible, hope of the Old Testament, heartbeat of the New.

John Proctor

Lifeline

An account of the genealogy of Jesus the Messiah, the son of David, the son of Abraham... So all the generations from Abraham to David are fourteen generations; and from David to the deportation to Babylon, fourteen generations; and from the deportation to Babylon to the Messiah, fourteen generations.

Matthew's Gospel is a book of hope. That is why it begins by looking back. God has worked in the past. For God, time is not just an endlessly unrolling carpet. It is a world of purpose and promise, a road with landmarks, direction and a destination.

Jesus was born into a line of hope: 'the Messiah, the son of David, the son of Abraham'. Abraham was the father of the people of Israel. God had promised that Abraham's children would bless the whole world (Genesis 12:3). In Jesus the blessing was about to be released and to reach the nations.

David had been Israel's greatest king, a sign of God's power and rule in the world. By Jesus' time, he was a remote memory, a rosy glow on the distant horizon of history, but Jesus was coming to stir that memory into new life, to show once again that God is king on earth.

Messiah means 'anointed', someone marked out by God for a special task. Jesus was a man on a mission, with gifts and responsibilities from God and work to do for God. The word *Messiah* comes from Hebrew, the language of the Old Testament; the New Testament word for 'anointed' is *Christ*. So 'Jesus Christ' is not just a name. It speaks about God's purpose and power at work in Jesus.

The genealogy in Matthew 1 splits into three sections. One of the dividing points is David, a high-water mark in Israel's history. The other divider is the exile to Babylon, which was a desperate and dismal low. There were peaks and valleys on the path that led to Jesus, yet all of it was gathered into Israel's journey of grace. Through the turbulence of time, God's purposes grow and ripen. As we enter Advent, we speak of hope and live in hope, because this is God's world.

Prayer

May the God of hope fill us with all joy and peace in believing, so that we may abound in hope by the power of the Holy Spirit.

Based on Romans 15:13

JP

Christmas presence

'Joseph, son of David, do not be afraid to take Mary as your wife, for the child conceived in her is from the Holy Spirit. She will bear a son, and you are to name him Jesus, for he will save his people from their sins.' All this took place to fulfil what had been spoken by the Lord through the prophet: 'Look, the virgin shall conceive and bear a son, and they shall name him Emmanuel', which means, 'God is with us.'

Often we take our names for granted. They were given to us long before we had any say in the matter. Generally they have a meaning, but we rarely pause to reflect on it, for a name is a label and, as we use it, it takes new life from the person to whom it belongs.

As Matthew tells of the birth of God's anointed one, we hear two names, both heavy with meaning. Certainly they gain fresh life from the one who carried them, but as we read this Gospel, they also give life to the story. They tell us what to expect and how to read between the lines of the events ahead.

'Name him Jesus,' says the angel to Joseph. Jesus is really a Hebrew word: *Yeshua* is probably the most exact way of writing it in English. It means 'God saves' or 'God to the rescue'. Jesus' birth is the launching of a rescue mission. He comes to undo the mess we have made of God's world, to 'save his people from their sins'. The Gospel story shows Jesus facing the tangles and trials of human life and sharing its pain and hurt. Dealing with sin is no casual or comfortable task. This is, from birth, a child of sorrows.

Then Matthew quotes a line from Isaiah (7:14), one of a dozen or so places where this Gospel speaks of the 'fulfilment' of an Old Testament text. The quotation ends with the name Emmanuel, again a Hebrew word, meaning 'God is with us'. This theme of presence is important in Matthew's Gospel. In Jesus, God lives among his people, and even when he leaves, he remains: 'Remember, I am with you always, to the end of the age' (Matthew 28:20).

Prayer

Lord Jesus, help me to remember your presence, to know that this world is not alone—and nor am I.

JP

Meeting of the Trinity

And when Jesus had been baptized, just as he came up from the water, suddenly the heavens were opened to him and he saw the Spirit of God descending like a dove and alighting on him. And a voice from heaven said, 'This is my Son, the Beloved, with whom I am well pleased.'

Matthew's Gospel introduces us to the adult Jesus at his baptism in the Jordan. This is the launching of his ministry, when he takes up the special work that God has for him. The Holy Spirit comes to touch him with God's power for the demands ahead. Just as the Spirit hovered like a dove over the waters (Genesis 1:2), shaping creation where all was formless and void, so here too God's Spirit comes as a creative force. Through Jesus the world will be remade and will discover more of its true and God-given wholeness.

The words from heaven ring with affirmation. God trusts Jesus and rejoices in him. Once again there are echoes of the Old Testament. Jesus takes up roles and expectations from his people's history and scripture. We overhear three different texts, which show Jesus in new light—and deep shadow.

First, there is an echo of Psalm 2:7, from a royal song about Israel's ancient kings. The kings represented God's presence among their people. At best, their rule was an expression of his. In a fuller and deeper way, Jesus is heaven's royal son, bringing God's kingdom near and making it more truly known.

The words 'beloved son' recall Genesis 22:2 and Abraham's near-sacrifice of Isaac. To speak of Jesus in these words is to see him too as a son of sacrifice, whose role will surely lead to distress and death.

Finally comes a line from the servant songs in Isaiah (42:1). The servant is utterly faithful to God, yet this will prove a costly and painful commitment. Only through his own pain will he bring help and hope to other people.

The experience of baptism both strengthens and challenges Jesus. God is with him in a new way, yet Jesus is set upon a lonely path, with no promise of ease or comfort as he goes. Is he ready? See tomorrow's reading.

Prayer

Lord Jesus Christ, share your strength with me when I have difficult work to do for God.

JP

MATTHEW 4:5–7 (NRSV)

Tested to destruction?

Then the devil took him to the holy city and placed him on the pinnacle of the temple, saying to him, 'If you are the Son of God, throw yourself down; for it is written, "He will command his angels concerning you", and "On their hands they will bear you up, so that you will not dash your foot against a stone."' Jesus said to him, 'Again it is written, "Do not put the Lord your God to the test."'

It's the sort of quip you might find on a fridge magnet: 'I can resist everything except temptation.' A more worldly wisdom says, 'Every person has a price.' We know that temptation can find us out very badly and that each of us has our weak points where we are most easily led off track. Jesus too was tempted, genuinely and searchingly (Hebrews 4:15).

'If you are the Son of God…' says the voice from below. Jesus has just heard that he is God's Son. The voice from heaven confirmed it (3:17). How could he doubt? But this temptation is not really about doubt. It is about the wrong kind of trust. The evil one wants Jesus to test his special status. Will he presume on God, put himself in a tight corner where God will have to intervene? The devil even turns to scripture. You can prove a lot of things from the Bible, if you take texts out of context.

Jesus is not so easily fooled. He knows his Bible too. The words he quotes come from Deuteronomy (6:16). Indeed, he uses Deuteronomy to answer all three of his temptations. In his own wilderness days he looks back to Israel's time in the desert. There the people learned the meaning of faith, and Jesus too means to trust God. The best way to prove the strength of a relationship is to live it, not constantly to test it.

So for us, living with God is a matter of trust. We can rely on God's goodness without measuring and proving it all the time. While God does not use his power wastefully, just to satisfy our curiosity, he will often use it generously to help us through difficulties and equip us for service.

Prayer

Lord Jesus, give me your wisdom, to resist temptation and to rejoice in trusting God.

JP

Light work

[Jesus] left Nazareth and made his home in Capernaum by the lake, in the territory of Zebulun and Naphtali, so that what had been spoken through the prophet Isaiah might be fulfilled: 'Land of Zebulun, land of Naphtali, on the road by the sea, across the Jordan, Galilee of the Gentiles—the people who sat in darkness have seen a great light, and for those who sat in the region and shadow of death light has dawned.' From that time Jesus began to proclaim, 'Repent, for the kingdom of heaven has come near.'

The lonely wilderness is behind and the busy communities of Galilee ahead. Jesus leaves the village where he grew up and settles in the little fishing port of Capernaum. From there he will go about Galilee, preaching and healing, gathering followers and teaching the ways of the kingdom.

First, though, Matthew mentions an Old Testament text about this area of Israel. It comes from Isaiah 9, a chapter about a prince of peace, who will restore God's kingdom of joy and justice. This, for Matthew, is surely half the point of using these verses: not just to talk about light in the north but to tell of God's rule. Jesus is a royal presence in the land, sent from God, empowered by God, bringing God near to the people.

Jesus' own message speaks of God's time. The kingdom has come near. This is a turning point in history, a critical moment in God's work, an opportunity for people to grasp. Jesus' call to 'repent' asks for a turning of life, an active commitment to the movement and way of living that he makes known. The kingdom must be grasped with a person's whole being; it is not a matter of the head alone.

In this way, light comes to Galilee. By the things Jesus does and the lifestyle he teaches, he illuminates his neighbours' world and opens their eyes to God. 'You are the light of the world,' he told his followers (Matthew 5:14). Still, today, he wants his people to bring clarity and brightness to our own corner of the world, by following his ways in our lives.

Prayer

Lord God, light of the minds that know thee, help us so to know thee that we may truly love thee.

Augustine of Hippo

JP

Storm before the calm

And when [Jesus] got into the boat, his disciples followed him. A gale arose on the lake, so great that the boat was being swamped by the waves; but he was asleep. And they went and woke him up, saying, 'Lord, save us! We are perishing!' And he said to them, 'Why are you afraid, you of little faith?' Then he got up and rebuked the winds and the sea; and there was a dead calm. They were amazed, saying, 'What sort of man is this, that even the winds and the sea obey him?'

The Sea of Galilee is really just an inland lake, but it is oval in shape, so that the middle is a few miles from the nearest shore. Some of Jesus' disciples fished this water. They knew its winds and its ways. They must have wished they had never started this voyage, that they had stayed on home ground instead of crossing to the Gentile side of the lake.

This is one of a series of miracles in Matthew 8 and 9—about ten altogether. Jesus moves around Galilee, bringing health and wholeness to troubled lives. He spreads peace and kindles faith. Many of the incidents contain a message about Jesus himself: who is he; why does he forgive; where does he get his power? Dawn breaks in people's minds as they start to ask the right questions about him.

This stilling of the storm certainly made the disciples think. The lake was their territory, they worked here, and yet they had been very scared. Then Jesus handled the situation and settled the water. As the Spirit once brought order and beauty out of chaos (Genesis 1:1–2), so Jesus too set wild elements to rest. The powers that shaped creation seemed to be at work through him. He spoke calm to the stormy waters, just as he brought peace to turbulent human lives.

God's presence was in Jesus and God's power was active in him too—a gentle, steadying power, helping the world to come to rest and live at peace. Like the disciples, we may get out of our depth, even in situations we thought we could handle, but we are never out of range of Jesus' strength and care.

For reflection
Even 'little faith' (v. 26) can ask for help from a great God.

JP

111

Take me to your...

Then Jesus went about all the cities and villages, teaching in their synagogues, and proclaiming the good news of the kingdom, and curing every disease and every sickness. When he saw the crowds, he had compassion for them, because they were harassed and helpless, like sheep without a shepherd. Then he said to his disciples, 'The harvest is plentiful, but the labourers are few; therefore ask the Lord of the harvest to send out labourers into his harvest.'

Just as Israel is full of flocks of sheep, so her scriptures are full of shepherds. In book after book of the Old Testament we meet shepherds at work. Often, God is called a shepherd of his people. In other places the shepherd is a picture of leadership, of the king or of people who carry religious responsibility. Shepherding is an image of control and care. The shepherd is in charge but must also be alert to the welfare and condition of the flock, noticing what they need and how they are coping.

When the crowds around Jesus are called 'sheep without a shepherd', this is a message about leadership. There is a vacuum where there should be care and guidance. A job is waiting to be done. Jesus longs to offer his people the leadership they need and to guide them with the wisdom and compassion of God.

Then the image changes, from shepherding to harvest. 'We need workers,' says Jesus, 'to go and gather people in. Pray for them.' Jesus does not plan to win the world—or even to win Galilee—by his activity alone. He wants messengers who will speak for him and help others to discover his shepherd care.

So Jesus started with the Twelve, sending them 'to the lost sheep of the house of Israel' (10:6). Later, at the end of the Gospel, as he leaves his friends, he says, 'Go.' Still, the Church prays and goes in his name, gathering the harvest, making the shepherd known. As we ponder our own place in this mission, we may feel unworthy to share in Jesus' work, but remember that our first duty is to pray. If we pray, God will surely send.

Prayer

In our time, Lord Jesus, may many find your shepherd care. Give the Church a desire to make you known, and people who can do it well.

JP

MATTHEW 11:2–6 (NRSV)

Actions speak

When John heard in prison what the Messiah was doing, he sent word by his disciples and said to him, 'Are you the one who is to come, or are we to wait for another?' Jesus answered them, 'Go and tell John what you hear and see: the blind receive their sight, the lame walk, the lepers are cleansed, the deaf hear, the dead are raised, and the poor have good news brought to them. And blessed is anyone who takes no offence at me.'

These verses sum up all that Jesus has done in Galilee. His mission has been one of work and word, of message and action. He has taught (Matthew 5—7) and he has healed, on many occasions and among many different needs (Matthew 8—9). Through him the love of God has been open to the varied faces of human sorrow and hurt. His healings have been signs of good news, and his preaching has brought a message of wholeness to bruised lives.

As often in Matthew, these verses resonate with scripture. We overhear the text in Isaiah 61 that Jesus used in the synagogue at Nazareth (Luke 4:16–21): 'The Spirit of the Lord is upon me, for he has anointed me to bring good news to the poor.' We catch too an echo of Isaiah 35:5–6: 'Then the eyes of the blind shall be opened, and the ears of the deaf un-stopped; then the lame shall leap like a deer.' Jesus says, in effect, 'You ask who I am. Just look:

promises are being fulfilled; lives are blessed; God is bringing salva-tion to his people. Let that be answer enough.'

It may seem odd that John the Baptist wondered about Jesus and needed to ask whether he really was the Messiah—but John was in prison. Pressure, tiredness and fear do hard things to the human spirit. If we are severely pressed by life, our faith too may get knocked out of shape. We may need to be reassured about things we once knew well. This chapter does not criticize John. It invites him to grasp afresh what God is doing and, although he cannot share in it, to rejoice and give praise.

For prayer

Remember anyone you know who is burdened by difficult circumstances. Ask God to reassure them, to keep their faith secure and steady.

JP

Eyes of a child

At that time Jesus said, 'I thank you, Father, Lord of heaven and earth, because you have hidden these things from the wise and the intelligent and have revealed them to infants; yes, Father, for such was your gracious will. All things have been handed over to me by my Father; and no one knows the Son except the Father, and no one knows the Father except the Son and anyone to whom the Son chooses to reveal him.'

A delightful snippet appeared in the press a few years ago. It concerned a local authority in Switzerland—a land fabled for efficiency and punctuality. This town council kept computer records of all its inhabitants and every year at the appointed time they took from the computer the names of children due to start primary school. Then they wrote to the parents with information about the arrangements. At the start of 1999, they wrote to all those whose birth date was '93, the rising six-year-olds, to invite them to start school. A few days later a letter arrived at the municipal offices from a lady in the town: 'Dear Sir or Madam, Thank you for your letter. However, since my father has recently attained the age of a hundred and five, he does not intend to enrol in your esteemed primary school.'

No doubt that local authority now lists the hundreds column in its birth records, and not just the tens and units—but there is something in this story that matches today's reading from Matthew. Jesus' words make infants of us all. However far we have travelled, there are things we shall never grasp by experience alone. Indeed, if experience and learning make us too sure of ourselves, they will close our eyes to the gospel.

With the Christian good news, we can only see clearly through the eyes of a child. With the Messiah, the world is always a fresh place. There is much to learn, more to discover. We do not unearth the secrets of life by our own ingenuity but we receive the insight to live, as a gift of God, revealed in Jesus. In the foolishness and mystery of a carpenter on a cross is all the wisdom of heaven.

Prayer

God of the cross, attract us by your truth and help us to understand you with humble hearts and clear eyes.

JP

Just gentleness

The Pharisees went out and conspired against him, how to destroy him. When Jesus became aware of this, he departed. Many crowds followed him, and he cured all of them, and he ordered them not to make him known. This was to fulfil what had been spoken through the prophet Isaiah: 'Here is my servant, whom I have chosen, my beloved, with whom my soul is well pleased. I will put my Spirit upon him, and he will proclaim justice to the Gentiles. He will not wrangle or cry aloud, nor will anyone hear his voice in the streets.'

People in Jesus' time had various ideas about God's Messiah. Some expected a figure of power, a leader who could assert his strength in the land. Jesus adopted a gentler style. He would not avoid controversy if it arose but he certainly did not welcome conflict for its own sake. Here we see him on the move, seeking new opportunities to teach and heal rather than picking an early quarrel with his enemies.

As Jesus healed, he urged people not to publicize his work. He could do without the wrong kind of PR. This, says Matthew, fits exactly the profile of God's servant in the prophecy of Isaiah (42:1–4), for the servant's quietness and gentleness match Jesus' approach to needs and situations. Jesus loves to go among people and meet them, but he does not advertise his whereabouts to the world. He speaks quietly and personally with individuals, giving people room to respond rather than imposing himself upon them.

The Isaiah quotation mentions 'justice to the Gentiles'. There the servant figure offers to the world the justice of Israel's God. In Matthew's Gospel we do not meet many Gentiles, yet Jesus' ministry moves constantly and steadily towards the time when the Church will go out from Israel to the nations. The gentleness of the servant will turn out to be a costly strategy, but, in suffering, Jesus will open the way to all the earth's peoples. The word of the cross will be a message for the world.

For reflection

Gentleness is not always the way of the world. In some spheres of life, recognition comes by force and strength or through attending to image. Review the way you live. Are there situations in which you might start to be more like Jesus?

JP

God only knows

Now when Jesus came into the district of Caesarea Philippi, he asked his disciples, 'Who do people say that the Son of Man is?' And they said, 'Some say John the Baptist, but others Elijah, and still others Jeremiah or one of the prophets.' He said to them, 'But who do you say that I am?' Simon Peter answered, 'You are the Messiah, the Son of the living God.' And Jesus answered him, 'Blessed are you, Simon son of Jonah! For flesh and blood has not revealed this to you, but my Father in heaven.'

This is a major turning point in the Gospel. The cross is about to come into view. Shortly Jesus will commit himself to the journey to Jerusalem and to the suffering that waits for him there (16:21). As he goes, Matthew's readers know, and his disciples know too, that he is truly the Messiah and Son of God.

Caesarea Philippi was right on the edge of the holy land, well to the north of Galilee. The town was named after the Roman emperor Augustus Caesar, and a shrine was there to the Greek god Pan. There, amid gods and lords of the Gentile world, Jesus asks his disciples what they make of him. Public opinion had been pretty varied—it often is—but Peter had sensed the truth. Jesus was the anointed Son of the God of Israel.

There is an Old Testament echo in 2 Samuel 7:12–16. There God promised David a royal successor, who would reign for ever as God's son, and Peter's words point to Jesus as this king. He is the one whose rule will never cease. In him the ancient promise takes flesh and the future becomes a place of hope and possibility.

Only God could have brought Peter to the point of grasping this. Faith is a gift and a blessing, never just a human understanding. 'Who do you say that I am?' is not a question we can resolve by study or thought or ability on their own. When we want to understand things that only God knows, humility, prayer and discipleship are necessary, too.

Prayer

God of wisdom and goodness, please give me a mind open to your truth, a heart receptive to your love and a spirit humble before your greatness.

JP

High point of faith

Six days later, Jesus took with him Peter and James and his brother John and led them up a high mountain, by themselves. And he was transfigured before them, and his face shone like the sun, and his clothes became dazzling white. Suddenly there appeared to them Moses and Elijah, talking with him. Then Peter said to Jesus, 'Lord, it is good for us to be here; if you wish, I will make three dwellings here, one for you, one for Moses, and one for Elijah.'

The transfiguration of Jesus comes just after Peter's statement of faith, and after Jesus' words about his suffering ahead. It confirms, visually and splendidly, who Jesus is. The prospect of the cross does not rub out his relationship with God. As he goes to die, the glory of heaven and the witness of scripture gather around him.

Moses and Elijah speak for the saints and witnesses of the Old Testament. Moses had been Israel's lawgiver and Elijah one of the boldest of the prophets. Both had met God on a mountain at times of crisis and testing for them and for the people (Exodus 33:17–23; 1 Kings 19). Both had experienced the glory of God (Exodus 34:29–35; 2 Kings 2:11). Furthermore, Elijah was expected to return to prepare the way for the coming of God. He would be a herald of peace and of a new dawn (Malachi 4:5–6).

In different ways these two figures from the past speak of God's continuing involvement in Israel's life. Here on the mountain, heaven and earth stand open one to another. Past and present speak together; history and hope connect. For a moment the three disciples glimpse the spread of God's loving purpose and the way that this finds focus in Jesus.

Peter means well with his offer to build three shelters, but you cannot freeze-frame encounters with God. High points are given to sustain us, to move us to worship, to teach us awe and perspective and trust. When the moment passes, we can be truly faithful only by coming down from the mountain and getting on with the journey ahead.

Prayer

God of glory and of history, keep us confident in your power and purpose, so that we do not need to dwell in the past but can trust you for the future.

JP

Cup winners?

Then the mother of the sons of Zebedee came to him with her sons, and kneeling before him, she asked a favour of him. And he said to her, 'What do you want?' She said to him, 'Declare that these two sons of mine will sit, one at your right hand and one at your left, in your kingdom.' ... [Jesus] said to them, 'You will indeed drink my cup, but to sit at my right hand and at my left, this is not mine to grant, but it is for those for whom it has been prepared by my Father.'

Parents love to see their children do well. It is a natural desire, and this support can encourage a young person to develop their gifts and confidence, but occasionally a parent's ambitions do more harm than good. It is hard to see straight when your own child's success is involved, yet too much of the wrong kind of encouragement can mislead badly.

Today's reading is an encounter of the wrong kind. No doubt James and John were as keen as their mother to push themselves to the head of the queue, to be the best disciples of the Twelve. They missed the point of following Jesus, however. Suffering is at the heart of his mission; this is the sort of Messiah he is. The 'cup' is an Old Testament image for God's anger and the suffering it brings (Isaiah 51:17, 22). Jesus called his own suffering a cup when he prayed in Gethsemane (Matthew 26:39), and at the last supper he used a cup to symbolize the shedding of his blood (26:27–28).

James and John would be cup winners of that kind. Both would suffer for Jesus: John was beaten for preaching the gospel; James was executed (Acts 5:40; 12:2). Neither would find an easy path of discipleship and surely they stopped expecting it after Jesus was crucified. Their mother, too, as she waited at the cross (Matthew 27:55–56), saw Jesus and his kingdom in a different light.

We love to see members of our families doing well. Maybe this story reminds us that faithfulness matters more than fortune.

Prayer

God of the cross, thank you for all you have taken on yourself of the world's sorrow and sin. Please give us the courage to take up the cross with you.

JP

MATTHEW 25:31–40 (NRSV, ABRIDGED)

You will find me

'When the Son of Man comes in his glory... he will separate people one from another as a shepherd separates the sheep from the goats... Then the king will say to those at his right hand, "Come, you that are blessed by my Father, inherit the kingdom prepared for you from the foundation of the world; for I was hungry and you gave me food, I was thirsty and you gave me something to drink, I was a stranger and you welcomed me, I was naked and you gave me clothing, I was sick and you took care of me, I was in prison and you visited me... Truly I tell you, just as you did it to one of the least of these who are members of my family, you did it to me."'

As the Gospel moves towards the cross, Jesus' final piece of teaching is this solemn parable. It takes our eyes beyond the suffering to the glory that is ahead and it acts as a window in the Gospel story, for the challenge of these words comes off the page into our lives.

Here are a host of Gospel themes. There is hope: Jesus is the glorious Son of Man and earth's deeds will be judged under his searching eye. Then comes an image from everyday life: Jesus notices in the work of a shepherd a picture of the work of God. Third, there is a serious emphasis on practical action: faith without deeds is dead (James 2:26), and Jesus wanted people's faith to be lively and active. Finally we see Jesus' special care for the troubled and the trodden-upon of the world.

This parable sets the scene for the crucifixion. The Christ of the cross identifies with little people. If we come to the cross for salvation, we shall be sent out in service, and this will take us time and again to hurting people and humble places. There Jesus will be waiting, caring for that situation more than we do and meeting us where we did not expect him. The Messiah of scripture, the Christ of Christmas, is the Son of Man whom we find when we support the lowly and serve the loveless.

Prayer

Lord Jesus Christ, give us eyes to see, hearts to care, hands to serve, for your sake.

JP

Fight, flight or fruit?

Many peoples shall come and say, 'Come, let us go up to the mountain of the Lord, to the house of the God of Jacob; that he may teach us his ways and that we may walk in his paths.' For out of Zion shall go forth instruction, and the word of the Lord from Jerusalem. He shall judge between the nations, and shall arbitrate for many peoples; they shall beat their swords into ploughshares, and their spears into pruning hooks; nation shall not lift up sword against nation, neither shall they learn war any more. O house of Jacob, come, let us walk in the light of the Lord!

When it comes to 'fight or flight', I'm among the frontrunners of the 'fleers'. I will go a long way to avoid confrontation, even though confrontation is sometimes necessary for the sake of justice. Some say that there are three options when we are confronted by potential hostility: fight, flight or freeze. I can identify with the 'freeze' option, too. When the going gets tough, sometimes all I can do is sit like a frightened rabbit in the glare of the headlights of the oncoming car.

So it is with real joy that I discover in today's word of peace that God offers us a very different view of what 'peace' might mean when we find ourselves in confrontation situations. It's about the promise that 'they shall beat their swords into ploughshares and their spears into pruning hooks'. This is a vision of peace that is at once profoundly simple and enormously difficult to embrace.

To take up the ploughshare and the pruning hook in place of the sword and spear is to go beyond the 'fight' option, but also to stand firm in the right place, without either 'fleeing' or 'freezing'. It is an invitation to turn the destructive energy of aggression into the creative energy of drawing fruitfulness from the situation.

It takes courage to choose this path and it takes wisdom. We don't have too much of either of these, but we know their source— the One who waits to teach us his ways, to bring genuine justice into our lives and to shed his light on our darkest emotions.

Reflection

Fighting, fleeing, freezing or fruit bearing? Which will we choose next time things get tough?

MS

Let God take the strain

Surely, this commandment that I am commanding you today is not too hard for you, nor is it too far away. It is not in heaven, that you should say, 'Who will go up to heaven for us, and get it for us so that we may hear it and observe it?' Neither is it beyond the sea, that you should say, 'Who will cross to the other side of the sea for us, and get it for us so that we may hear it and observe it? No, the word is very near to you; it is in your mouth and in your heart for you to observe…. Today… I have set before you life and death, blessings and curses. Choose life so that you and your descendants may live, loving the Lord your God, obeying him, and holding fast to him.

How do you unwind when you've been overdoing things? Maybe you have a soak in a warm bath or take a walk or curl up with a good book? Probably it is something that releases the strain of anxious activity, allowing you simply to be.

So much of our life is actually lived under strain, torn between regret for the past and anxiety for the future. Strain pulls us out of joint. It's strain that makes things break.

Today's word of peace invites us to stop straining. This is especially hard in the week before Christmas —especially hard and especially necessary! Today we are invited to stop straining up to the highest heavens to find God, to stop straining across the farthest seas to hear his word. We don't even have to strain our eyes and our ears. The word is closer to us than our next breath. It is in our hearts—but to hear it we need to come to stillness and be totally immersed in the present moment.

Try entering this deep stillness today, even if just for a few minutes. Know that in the deep centre of your own heart you are in the presence of the living God, who urges you to 'choose life'—the life that only God can give, which he has already planted deep within your own heart.

Reflection

'Take from our souls the strain and stress and let our ordered lives confess the beauty of thy peace.'

John Greenleaf Whittier (1807–92)

MS

Asleep in God's lap

O Lord, my heart is not lifted up, my eyes are not raised too high;
I do not occupy myself with things too great and too marvellous for
me. But I have calmed and quieted my soul, like a weaned child
with its mother; my soul is like the weaned child that is with me.
O Israel, hope in the Lord from this time on and for evermore.

It was the evening of the Christmas concert and our local concert hall was packed to the rafters. I settled down and relaxed in my seat, looking forward to an enjoyable evening.

Immediately in front of me on the tiered theatre seats was a small boy, who clearly wasn't looking forward to this treat as much as I was. He fidgeted continuously and shuffled around in his seat, and with every restless move his head jolted against my knees. I was beginning to lose patience and my attention was focused more on this child than on the concert itself.

Then a strange thing happened. He suddenly went over his tiredness threshold. His little head slid back, came to rest on my knees, and he was asleep. What was strange wasn't the fact of his falling asleep, but the effect it had on me. Suddenly, from one minute to the next, this fidgety child who had been irritating me so much had turned into a little person who trusted me enough to fall asleep, resting his head on my lap.

From then on, my irritation melted into tender solicitude and care to make sure that my knees provided a gentle pillow for him. I was deeply aware of his sleeping presence and I enjoyed the concert more than I could possibly have hoped. Both he and I had found a place of peace.

It's a memory that lives on in my heart. I think of it especially when I read this psalm. In my prayer I ask God's permission to fall asleep in his lap, and all is well. Not that we need permission, of course. If we feel so privileged when a little child rests in our arms, how much more might God rejoice over one who was restless and now has come to a place of peace?

Reflection

*Let God simply cradle you today
in the arms of love.*

MS

Too many 'Yes's?

Now as [Jesus and his disciples] went on their way, he entered a certain village, where a woman named Martha welcomed him into her home. She had a sister named Mary, who sat at the Lord's feet and listened to what he was saying. But Martha was distracted by her many tasks; so she came to him and asked, 'Lord, do you not care that my sister has left me to do all the work by myself? Tell her then to help me.' But the Lord answered her, 'Martha, Martha, you are worried and distracted by many things; there is need of only one thing. Mary has chosen the better part, which will not be taken away from her.'

It had been a really busy week. Events had overtaken our intention to take a short break over the weekend, and I was thoroughly in 'Martha mode'.

In this state of mind I visited a sick friend. He asked about our holiday. I admitted that it hadn't happened and told him all the pressing reasons why we hadn't been able to get away. He listened in silence. I was expecting him to remind me of how important it is to relax, but instead he said something that stunned and shocked me, and that I have never forgotten.

'Too many "yes"s,' he said, 'sometimes conceal a deeper "no!"'

I felt the tears rising. This friend knew me well and he was wise enough to perceive what my 'deeper no' might be about. For a moment he was speaking to my heart as Jesus spoke to Martha's heart, and I wondered whether Martha had felt as totally known, yet as deeply loved, as I did myself at that moment.

Since then I have often stopped myself amid all my 'yes-saying' to ask 'What is this busyness really all about? How much of it is coming from a genuine desire to serve and how much is about avoiding things I would rather not look at in myself?'

God is love, and the challenge to be still in his presence and let go of our busyness is offered to us in infinite tenderness, by the one who knows exactly what is stirring in our hearts.

Reflection

Explore with God some of your own 'yes's and let him gently open up any underlying 'no's.

MS

Thursday 20 December

MATTHEW 8:18, 23–27 (NRSV)

Peace in the eye of the storm

Now when Jesus saw great crowds around him, he gave orders to go over to the other side... And when he got into the boat, his disciples followed him. A gale arose on the lake, so great that the boat was being swamped by the waves; but he was asleep. And they went and woke him up, saying, 'Lord, save us! We are perishing!' And he said to them, 'Why are you afraid, you of little faith?' Then he got up and rebuked the winds and the sea; and there was a dead calm. They were amazed, saying, 'What sort of man is this, that even the winds and the sea obey him?'

I've never personally experienced the power of a hurricane, although I've watched its effects on television. What always amazes me is that right at the heart of such destructive force, there is a still centre. If you could stand in this still centre, the storm would rage all around you but not a hair on your head would be disturbed by it.

It's very hard to remember this when we find ourselves being tossed around by the kind of storms that afflict us day by day— stormy situations at work or stormy passages in difficult relationships or the storms that brew up within our own hearts in the endless conflict between the best and the worst within us. What is true in nature is true in the spiritual journey, too. At the deep heart of the stormiest situation, there is a still centre where we are held in the heart of God. In that still centre, and in no other place, will we discover the way forward and draw on the resources we need to make the next step.

What does that still centre mean for you? Perhaps a quiet corner where you can pray or an abiding memory of how God has been with you in other stormy times?

Just as Jesus slept in the storm-tossed boat on the waters of Galilee, so God rests eternally in the heart of our own life's storms. We can struggle on alone, trying to stay afloat, or we can turn to him as his first friends did.

Reflection

How is the weather in your life right now? Is it time to wake the Lord?

MS

The peace of presence

[Jesus said] 'I have said these things to you while I am still with you. But the Advocate, the Holy Spirit, whom the Father will send in my name, will teach you everything, and remind you of all that I have said to you. Peace I leave with you; my peace I give to you. I do not give to you as the world gives. Do not let your hearts be troubled, and do not let them be afraid. You heard me say to you, "I am going away, and I am coming to you." If you loved me, you would rejoice that I am going to the Father, because the Father is greater than I. And now I have told you this before it occurs, so that when it does occur, you may believe.'

An exhausted parent finally sits down to relax after getting a fractious child off to bed and to sleep. War-weary soldiers finally board the plane to fly back home after being embroiled in conflict for months. A politician comes down from the hustings after arguing all day with his opponent and finally winning the vote. They all think they have reached 'peace'.

But the fractious child will wake again. The conflict will break out again. The political opponent will come back to fight another day.

Jesus turns all our thoughts of 'peace' on their heads. He tells us that his peace is something quite different. Our 'peace' is about absence: the absence of disturbance or conflict or trouble. God's peace is about presence: God's own unfailing presence in every moment of our living.

Nothing in the world can give us this deep peace of presence, but nothing in the world can ever take it away from us either.

When have you known—really known in your heart—the peace that only God can give? For most of us, such moments are rare, but they are the signs of a presence that is always there, whether we are aware of it or not. Remember any moments like this and savour them in your prayer today.

Reflection

To have known just one moment of the peace of God's eternal presence is to know that it is always there, just as the sun always shines even though the clouds may temporarily hide its light.

MS

Unlikely friendships

A shoot shall come out from the stock of Jesse, and a branch shall grow out of his roots. The spirit of the Lord shall rest on him, the spirit of wisdom and understanding, the sprit of counsel and might, the spirit of knowledge and the fear of the Lord... The wolf shall live with the lamb, the leopard shall lie down with the kid, the calf and the lion and the fatling together, and a little child shall lead them... They will not hurt or destroy on all my holy mountain; for the earth will be full of the knowledge of the Lord as the waters cover the sea.

This sounds like a parallel universe! Surely such peace and harmony don't exist on planet earth. Yet, amazingly, there are creatures among us now who can show us something about how such harmony might really begin to happen.

Take the buffalo, for instance. You really wouldn't want to run into a buffalo on a dark night. Their massive bulk and intimidating appearance, complete with horns, doesn't immediately suggest a warm welcome. But they have a friend—a tiny colourful bird called the oxpecker, who thinks nothing of landing on the buffalo's nose for a meal of ticks, flies and maggots, and bringing its host welcome relief from these parasites.

You wouldn't want to tangle with a crocodile if you value your life, but another bird, the thick-knee, actually enjoys sitting among the crocodile's teeth! It lives on the parasites there and the crocodile gets a visit to the dental hygienist for free.

These are symbiotic relationships—relationships between unlikely companions, each of whom benefits from the encounter—and they have something to teach us. When we live and work for the welfare of each other, as well as just our own, a whole new range of possibilities opens up and natural fears and enmities can be dissolved.

The time will come, the prophet tells us, when this will be the norm for our world—and the one who heralds that perfect peace, and will teach us how to live towards it, is already springing forth from the stock of Jesse.

Reflection

Every act of loving service dissolves a little of the hard rock of distrust and enmity.

MS

Incarnation

Two thousand years ago, Jesus was born, almost unnoticed, amid the hustle of the Roman census in Bethlehem. In two days' time, we celebrate his birth again amid the bustle of presents, parties and diet-breaking! Perhaps Jesus will go unnoticed still, but the truth does not need an audience; he was Emmanuel (God with us) then and he is still with us now. This is the incarnation—the astonishing, amazing initiative of God the Creator, who entered into his creation as a human being, as one of the created. The question is: why did he do this?

Jesus gave an answer when he said: 'Do not think that I have come to abolish the Law or the Prophets; I have not come to abolish them but to fulfil them' (Matthew 5:17, TNIV). If we think of 'the Law' as the Ten Commandments, we think that Jesus will fulfil it through his actions (by doing). In Hebrew thought, however, 'the Law' meant the law of Moses (the first five books of the Bible, the Pentateuch) and 'the Prophets' meant the rest of the Old Testament. So Jesus did not say that he would fulfil the Commandments. He said that he would fulfil Genesis, Exodus, Leviticus, Numbers, Deuteronomy and so forth (and 'fulfil' also means 'complete, perfect and accomplish'). What if Jesus fulfilled the scriptures incarnately (by being)? Is it possible for him to embody the law, to be the Pentateuch incarnate?

It helps to understand that 'the Law' doesn't just mean rules. The Pentateuch contains rules (laws) but it also describes God's dealings with his creation through his relationship with particular individuals. Adam, Noah, Abraham, Moses, Levi and Joshua are just six of the key people whom God related to and through. If Jesus is the embodiment of the Pentateuch, it means that what God began through Adam, Abraham, Moses and the others is completed, perfected, fulfilled and accomplished in him.

For the next nine days, we shall lift the Christmas tinsel and focus on Jesus. He is the embodiment of God's promise. He is God's Word spoken in the language of humanity. That's the depth and simplicity of incarnation: human beings understand and apprehend the spiritual through the physical. Incarnation is about God being here with us, in the thick of human life. Let's not allow the celebration of Christmas to camouflage the reality of what God has done.

David Robertson

In the beginning

So God created human beings in his own image, in the image of God he created them; male and female he created them. God blessed them and said to them, 'Be fruitful and increase in number; fill the earth and subdue it. Rule over the fish in the sea and the birds in the sky and over every living creature that moves on the ground.' ... God saw all that he had made, and it was very good.

The creation accounts begin the five books of the law. They teach various truths about God, life on earth and the human race. According to Genesis, human beings are unique in terms of their 'method' of creation and their role within it. For example, when God creates light and sky, he does so by his word (1:3, 6). When he creates vegetation and livestock, he commands the existing creation to 'produce' this new life (vv. 11, 24). When it comes to human beings, though, Genesis 1 speaks of God creating the race in his own image, and chapter 2 describes him reaching into the creation, making a body from some of the 'stuff' of life and then breathing his own Spirit into it. Therefore, human beings are a fusion of earth and heaven, beings that are both flesh and spirit.

According to their 'being', the race is given a role: to steward God's creation. It is not God's intention to oversee all that he has made; this will be done by human beings, who have, as it were, one foot in the creation and the other in the presence of God. Thus, from the very beginning, God deals 'incarnationally' with the earth— in and through the bodies of human beings. This is the pattern of creation, and it is 'very good'.

When Jesus was born and God became a human being, we rightly regard this as a 'new thing', but it is not a 'new pattern'. God has always, right from the beginning, related incarnationally with his creation. The difference is that now God has taken the original pattern and entered into it himself. Instead of relating to his creation through the human race, now he relates to the human race through one human being—Jesus.

Reflection

Veiled in flesh the Godhead see!
Hail the incarnate Deity!

Charles Wesley (1707–88) and others
DR

The first Adam

And the Lord God said, 'The man has now become like one of us, knowing good and evil. He must not be allowed to reach out his hand and take also from the tree of life and eat, and live for ever.' So the Lord God banished him from the Garden of Eden to work the ground from which he had been taken. After he drove them out, he placed on the east side of the Garden of Eden cherubim and a flaming sword flashing back and forth to guard the way to the tree of life.

Genesis 3 tells the story of human disobedience and the consequences for both human beings and for God. Until this point, Adam and Eve occupied their unique role in the creation as stewards. They were, themselves, the 'gateway' between God and the rest of the creation: if they turned one way, they were dealing with the earth; if they turned the other way, they were openly in the presence of God. Now, though, because of their disobedience, they are banished from this unimpeded relationship and an angel guards the gate. Now they must make their way within the creation as if they were of the same 'nature' as vegetation or livestock—just other creatures. At heart, this explains the human sense that 'Life shouldn't be like this!' No, it shouldn't, but the consequence of sin means that this is where and how we must live.

For God, the sin of the human race means that the original pattern of creation is blown apart. He, too, has lost his open relationship with human beings; he has also lost his stewards. If the creation is not stewarded spiritually, what will happen to it? The answer is an incarnate one: the human race will rule the creation and they will end up destroying it and each other. This is the flip side of incarnation: bodies created to live spiritually also implement spiritual ideas bodily. When the spirit is corrupt, the bodily deeds are devastating (Matthew 15:19).

Christmas celebrations tend to promise paradise but reflect reality. When Christmas is a letdown, it's a reminder that humanity needs help—which is why Jesus came.

Reflection

The hopes and fears of all the years are met in thee tonight.

Bishop Phillips Brooks (1835–93)

DR

The first and second manger

So Joseph also went up from the town of Nazareth in Galilee to Judea, to Bethlehem the town of David, because he belonged to the house and line of David. He went there to register with Mary, who was pledged to be married to him and was expecting a child. While they were there, the time came for the baby to be born, and she gave birth to her firstborn, a son. She wrapped him in cloths and placed him in a manger, because there was no guest room available for them.

This is the incarnation, which fulfils, or completes, all that has gone before. This little boy is 'God with us' and the embodiment of the original pattern of creation. He is the new gateway into the presence of God (John 10:7) and the one who will steward the human race back into a relationship with the Creator. But how? The clue is there right from the beginning.

Educated as we are by nativity plays and Christmas cards, we know exactly what a manger looks like. It's a wooden box on legs, filled with straw... isn't it? Well, when Jesus was born, stables were usually part of the house (rather than a shed at the bottom of the garden). The room where the beasts spent their night had a wide shelf (the manger) built into one wall and their feed was spread out on this. In fact, Jewish people used the same word for the stone shelves in tombs where bodies, wrapped in grave clothes, were laid to rest.

When Mary wrapped her baby in cloths and laid him in a manger, she acted prophetically. Thirty-three years later, Jesus would be wrapped in a different cloth and laid in another manger (Mark 15:46) and, astonishingly, God was equally incarnate in the baby boy and the crucified man. When Jesus arose from the first manger, it was in the arms of his earthly mother; when he arose from the second manger, it was in the arms of his heavenly Father. In the first, Jesus began his incarnate life; in the second, eternal life in all its fullness is offered to every human being (John 10:10).

Reflection

Lo within the manger lies
he who built the starry skies.

Edward Caswall (1814–78)
DR

A second Adam

For as in Adam all die, so in Christ all will be made alive... The first man was of the dust of the earth, the second man is of heaven. As was the earthly man, so are those who are of the earth; and as is the heavenly man, so also are those who are of heaven. And just as we have borne the image of the earthly man, so shall we bear the image of the heavenly man.

The idea that Jesus is a second Adam is central to Paul's thinking about the incarnation, and the comparison between the two Adams is startling. The first Adam was given life but brought death to the human race; the second Adam accepted death and brought life. The first was barred from the presence of God; the second opened the way back. The first fathered a race lost to sin; the second dealt with sin so that all may be righteous.

If we think of history as 'linear', we misunderstand this teaching. Paul's understanding is that God did something 'circular' in Jesus: he somehow started again, as it were in the same place as the first Adam, but the second Adam chose obedience. The consequences of this, again, had implications for the whole race. Now there is an opportunity for every human being to begin again—not to try again but to be born again (John 3:7) with a new 'ancestor', Jesus, the second Adam.

This is an incarnate truth as Jesus, in his own body, takes to the cross the sin of every human body to create a new race (Ephesians 1:4–6). The original task of the human race was to steward the earth. That task remains, but another is added. The children of God are the body of Christ and share his task of seeking to steward the human race back into God's presence.

Christmas is often marked with parties, fun and sharing with friends and relatives. This is enjoyable and important but may have little to do with stewardship. Selfish consumption is a mark of the first Adam; selfless generosity is a mark of the second. God always chooses to work incarnately. What he began with Adam, he fulfilled in Jesus and wants to continue in us.

Reflection

Very God, begotten, not created.

J.F. Wade (1711–86),
tr. F Oakeley (1802–80)

DR

A second Noah

One day Jesus said to his disciples, 'Let us go over to the other side of the lake.' So they got into a boat and set out. As they sailed, he fell asleep. A squall came down on the lake, so that the boat was being swamped, and they were in great danger. The disciples went and woke him, saying, 'Master, Master, we're going to drown!' He got up and rebuked the wind and the raging waters; the storm subsided, and all was calm.

I wonder whether the last few days have been plain sailing—or has your Christmas been punctuated with gale force arguments and stormy waters? One of the key figures of the Pentateuch is Noah. His faith and obedience contrast sharply with the sin of humanity. When God decides to cleanse his creation, Noah is required to steward it (by building the ark and saving each species from extinction, including his own family). When the floodwaters subside, however, God makes it known that he will never again solve the problem of human sin in this way (Genesis 9:12–16). If Jesus is the embodiment (incarnation) of the Pentateuch (the law), then he is the second Adam, but is he also the second Noah?

It's good to look at today's reading through Old Testament eyes. On one level, this miracle scares the disciples rigid because, when Jesus calms the storm, he exhibits an authority over nature that belongs only to God. On another level, Jesus brings his disciples safely through the deep, stormy waters to dry land, saving from death those who would become the firstborn of the new race. Similarly, when Jesus saves Peter from drowning (Matthew 14:29–31), the incident is a living parable of personal salvation, a bodily event with a spiritual message (an incarnational truth).

If Jesus is a second Noah, then he does not need an ark. His own body becomes the 'vessel' of salvation so that all who are 'in Christ' are rescued from the flood of sin (Romans 8:1). The weather of life—or Christmas!—may be fair or foul but, on the cross, sin (not the sinner) is destroyed and Jesus embodies the promise of God made to Noah. He is the law incarnate.

Reflection

'God and sinners reconciled.'

Charles Wesley (1717–88) and others

DR

A second Abraham

[Christ] redeemed us in order that the blessing given to Abraham might come to the Gentiles through Christ Jesus, so that by faith we might receive the promise of the Spirit... The promises were spoken to Abraham and to his seed. Scripture does not say 'and to seeds', meaning many people, but 'and to your seed', meaning one person, who is Christ... So in Christ Jesus you are all children of God through faith... If you belong to Christ, then you are Abraham's seed, and heirs according to the promise.

When God calls Abraham and Sarah in Genesis 12, he promises to establish a new nation through them—even if they find this promise hard to believe. God intends this chosen people to have a particular relationship with their Creator and also to be a 'priestly nation' to the world (Exodus 19:5–6). In short, the whole nation will fill Adam's empty shoes, with one foot in the presence of God and the other in the creation.

The first point to note is that God chooses to create the nation organically. He doesn't commission an existing nation but grows a new one through Abraham, Sarah and their descendants. Second, he does not relate to his creation directly but through the Jewish people. They are the new gateway through which God relates to humanity and vice versa. This is incarnation, but the original pattern is reworked so that now it involves a nation rather than a race.

In Paul's thinking, Jesus, a descendant of Abraham, is the final outworking of this pattern of incarnation. Jesus is the founder of a new chosen nation of which all Christians are members (Ephesians 2:11–16) because now descent is traced spiritually, not physically. In this sense, Jesus is a second Abraham and the new nation, like the first, has different values. In many areas of life (including around Christmas-time), Christians may find themselves behaving in a different fashion from those around them, as they give thanks that the promises made to the first Abraham are fulfilled in Jesus and that they, regardless of birth or background, are family members and the heirs of every promise of God.

Reflection

He is alpha and omega,
he the source, the ending he.

Prudentius (348–413),
tr. J.M. Neale (1818–66)
DR

A second Moses

[The crowd] asked him, 'What sign then will you give that we may see it and believe you? What will you do? Our ancestors ate the manna in the wilderness; as it is written: "He gave them bread from heaven to eat."' Jesus said to them, 'Very truly I tell you, it is not Moses who has given you the bread from heaven, but it is my Father who gives you the true bread from heaven. For the bread of God is the bread that comes down from heaven and gives life to the world.'

When God sent Moses to confront Pharaoh and lead the Hebrew slaves out of Egypt, the incarnational pattern continued. God related to and through Moses. After various plagues, death visited every firstborn male in the land (Egyptian and Hebrew alike), but those who broke bread and smeared lamb's blood on their doorframes were spared—not because they were righteous but because they were obedient. In the desert, bread figured again when God fed the people with manna.

In subsequent generations, the Passover was celebrated in a meal with broken bread and shared toasts (Exodus 12:14). God's people looked back to the time when Moses freed them from slavery in Egypt and looked forward with expectation to the Messiah who would free them from their slavery to sin, restoring their relationship with God and the world.

When Jesus broke the Passover bread with his disciples, he embodied the role of both Messiah and the sacrificial firstborn male (Luke 22:19–20). When challenged to provide manna, Jesus pointed to himself (John 6:35). In Exodus, Moses gave the people bread but Jesus, the second Moses, is the bread. He is the fulfilment of God's promise of freedom from the old life and also the one who will sustain new life for eternity. He is able to free us from slavery to sin (John 8:34–36) and feed us each step of the way.

This Christmas, many families will have gone into debt in order to buy what amounts to bread sauce and turkey sandwiches. What a poor substitute for celebrating our freedom in the incarnation of God's living bread!

Reflection

O may we keep and ponder in our mind God's wondrous love in saving lost mankind.

J. Byrom (1692–1763)
DR

A second Levi

> When Christ came as high priest of the good things that are now already here, he went through the greater and more perfect tabernacle that is not made with human hands, that is to say, is not a part of this creation. He did not enter by means of the blood of goats and calves; but he entered the Most Holy Place once for all by his own blood, having obtained eternal redemption... For this reason Christ is the mediator of a new covenant.

Moses' brother Aaron was in charge of the rituals of the covenant. The Israelites traced priesthood through Aaron to Levi, and when they settled in the promised land, worship was centralized in the temple. It was the physical gateway into God's presence, with a curtain separating his dwelling place (the Most Holy Place) from the rest of the building. The priesthood acted as the spiritual gateway between God and his people, bringing his concerns to them and their concerns to him.

According to the writer of Hebrews, Jesus fulfilled (or completed) the covenant by embodying it. The lamb became the priest; the priest became the curtain; the curtain was ripped in two and the law became incarnate. In the old covenant, both temple and priesthood were incarnational in that God chose to work in and through them. In the new covenant, neither was abandoned; instead, they were completed. Both are incarnate in Christ, so Jesus is a second Levi as the expectations of the old covenant are fulfilled, or embodied, in him. The temple and priesthood are no longer relevant to the new race that 'descends' from Christ, because Christians are of the same 'family' as the new high priest. Just as every descendant of Levi was a priest, so every Christian shares Christ's priesthood and forms the new, living (incarnate) temple (1 Peter 2:5).

This Christmas, many people will visit their local church, but what will they find? A distant, old covenant God and an Old Testament priesthood standing between themselves and him? Or the new covenant high priest, Jesus, ministering directly in and through the New Testament temple—the body of Christ, the gathering of believers?

Reflection

*Suddenly the Lord descending
in his temple shall appear.*

J. Montgomery (1771–1854)
DR

A second Joshua

Jesus, full of the Holy Spirit, left the Jordan and was led by the Spirit into the wilderness, where for forty days he was tempted by the devil. He ate nothing during those days, and at the end of them he was hungry... Jesus returned to Galilee in the power of the Spirit, and news about him spread through the whole countryside. He taught in their synagogues, and everyone praised him.

Joshua is the bridge between the first five books of the Bible and the rest of the Old Testament. He is present with Moses in the desert but he is the leader who takes the Israelites into the promised land. Here kings and prophets will become the gateway people between God and the nation, with their lives forming the content of 'the Prophets' that Jesus fulfils, or embodies (Matthew 5:17).

God has always, from the beginning, related to his creation incarnationally, and nothing in the old covenant is abandoned; every aspect is incarnate in Christ. We have thought of Jesus as the second Adam, Noah, Abraham, Moses and Levi—and we could continue because Jesus, the ultimate king and prophet, is also a second David, Solomon, Samuel, Jeremiah and so on. Every aspect of the old covenant is embodied in him.

Today, however, we think about Joshua. After 40 years in the desert, he crossed the Jordan, Jericho was thrown down and God's chosen nation was established (Joshua 1 to 6). Jesus, after 40 days in the desert, also crossed the Jordan but was himself torn down to establish God's kingdom (Mark 14:58). Joshua led the nation into their promised land, but Jesus gathers into his kingdom believers from every nation (John 10:16). In the incarnate Christ, God once again did something 'circular', fulfilling every promise experienced through the first Joshua in the second: they even share the same name (the Greek version of Joshua, which means 'saviour', is Jesus)!

Tomorrow we begin a new year, and who knows what it will bring? The future may be wonderful, terrible or a mixture of the two, but as we cross over into 2008, who better to lead us than the second Joshua—Jesus, the promise of God incarnate?

Reflection

*Powers, dominions bow before him
and extol our God and King.*

Prudentius, tr. J.M. Neale

DR

The BRF

Magazine

Richard Fisher writes...

Open the Bible at random in a few places and you'll soon notice how many different types of writing it contains: poetry, prose, lists of names and numbers, dialogue and letters can all be found there. Some parts of it will draw you in immediately, while others may be frankly off-putting, at least at first sight.

At BRF, we've identified one of our core ministries as helping people to explore the Bible with confidence. All explorers going into unknown territory feel happier about the task if they have the right equipment—clothing and tools—to tackle every kind of environment they might encounter. BRF's books aim to do that for intrepid Bible readers—to make them equipped for all terrain.

This issue of the *BRF Magazine* kicks off with Henry Wansbrough's whistlestop tour of the whole Bible, spotlighting different parts in quick succession and providing insights into their origin and purpose. Later, Naomi Starkey suggests four ways of plotting a course through the various biblical books with the aid of the *People's Bible Commentary*. Whatever kind of journey you want to take, the PBC can provide you with a good map.

Not all explorers cover vast tracts of land, however, and exploring the Bible needn't mean trying to read the whole library that it contains. Naomi also recommends two books that focus more closely —one on the glory of Jesus in the Gospel of John and the other on what today's emerging church can learn from the first-century church at Antioch, home base for Paul's expeditions in the book of Acts.

We also have an extract from BRF's Advent book for 2007, discovering the 'beginnings and endings' encompassed by the Christian story, and a taster of Adrian Plass's revised and expanded edition of his bestselling collection of daily readings, *When You Walk*.

Finally, Lucy Moore gives us her insights into the excitement of opening up the special character of the Bible with primary school children, and explains how you can help with this huge task.

I hope you'll find something here to encourage you to set off on a new exploration of the Bible, confident that you're well equipped for whatever you discover on the journey.

Richard Fisher, Chief Executive

Bible salad

Henry Wansbrough OSB

I'm quite a serious sort of person, and when I read a book I like to learn something from it, something that helps me to understand a bit more about myself, my character and motivation, or about other people and their difficulties and achievements, or about the world and life in general. So I read a novel about an autistic child or about the difficulties that gradually poison a marriage. A biography will also do, to see how a general honed his skills or a bishop mastered his temper or a poet came to love the richness of life.

The Jews and early Christians collected many different sorts of writings that spoke to them about the ways of God. The Jews put them together and called them the Bible. The early Christians added more writings, which showed them what they considered to be the crowning end of the story. In one way it had already happened and in another it was still eagerly expected. All these writings added to their knowledge of God and of God's dealings with the world.

Even the writings of the New Testament show a great deal of variety. Don't open the New Testament without preparing for a bumpy ride! The writing starts, of course, with the letters that Paul wrote to various communities, all of which except the community at Rome, that awesome capital of empire, he had founded. To the Romans he shows great respect, as a provincial writing to the mighty city, hardly daring to offer them advice. To his much-loved community at Philippi (the only community from which he would accept gifts of money) he is affectionate and intimate. To his friend Philemon, the owner of his slave-helper Onesimus, he is playful and light-hearted, punning on Onesimus' name, which means 'Useful'. All of these were written long before the Gospels came into their present shape. After them come those two great letters, Colossians and Ephesians, which were perhaps not penned by Paul, but may be first fruits of his teaching and training, developing aspects of his own letters and applying his message to the situation of Christians a few years later.

At a certain stage, some community must have asked an unknown catechist named Mark to gather up and put together the oral traditions that had long been circulating in the communities. Why Mark? Because he was a brilliant storyteller, writing admittedly in primitive Greek, but with a sophisticated plan that brings out the charismatic personality of Jesus and the ever-increasing amazement of the people who could not help but see God at work in him. Soon afterward, two communities were not wholly satisfied with this portrait, wanting more of Jesus' teaching to be recorded. One, a community of Christians of Jewish origin, asked Matthew to give a fuller account against the background of Jesus' Jewish roots.

Another community, notably more affluent and settled in the milieu of the Greco-Roman empire, asked Luke to show them how Jesus and his message should be seen from their point of view. Luke had a genius for expressing a theological message through storytelling. Just look at the scene of the annunciation to Mary or the parable of the good Samaritan! He also wrote a second volume about the early years of the Christian community and about Paul's missionary journeys. This 'Acts of the Apostles' tells the story brilliantly, making the most of those favourite features of novels and histories of the time—riot scenes, escapes from prison, court appearances, shipwreck—not to mention the carefully worked speeches put into the mouths of the leading characters.

In a class by itself is the Gospel of John, seemingly almost entirely independent of the other Gospels, more developed theologically (but not necessarily therefore later). The 'beloved disciple' who stands behind this tradition dwells lovingly on the affection and human responsiveness of Jesus. The stories are fewer but are told with tranquillity and humour. Chiefly John struggles to show what it can mean to say that Jesus is fully divine. He has in every way the powers and dynamic of God. He is the Word of God made flesh.

In a class by itself is the Gospel of John

A wholly different sort of writing is strangely related to this author: the Revelation of John. It issues from the world of fierce persecution of Christians who would not join in the cult of the Roman emperors, assuring them—in the lurid symbolism of blood and cosmic collapse—that they would eventually triumph before the still higher throne of God and the Lamb.

If the types of writing in the New Testament are varied, those of the Old Testament are kaleidoscopic. Let us run backwards chronologically for a moment! The later writings range from the intense and agonized drama of Job's stalwart but trusting complaints at his undeserved suffering to the humorous novelette of the book of Tobit (in the Apocrypha), which at once honours and makes fun of the fussy exactitude of the old man's legal observance. The Wisdom literature ranges from the sage counsel and neat certainties of that learned scribe Ben Sira (again, Apocryphal) to the puzzled paradoxes of Qoheleth (Ecclesiastes), who poses as King Solomon himself. Even the prophets alone range from Isaiah's sublime and awe-inspired celebration of the Holy One of Israel to the self-critical humour of Jonah, the disobedient Jew who grumbles at God's acceptance of the obedience of the Gentiles. And in the Psalms all our own moods of prayer can be found, from dire complaint at unjustified (or, indeed, justified) persecution to tranquil or jubilantly noisy praise of the glory of God.

The backbone of the earlier part of the Old Testament is the history of God's gradual formation of his people of Israel, as he pats them into shape through thick and thin—and there is plenty of both. This account makes use of all kinds of material, from the oral folk-history of the patriarchs, half-lost in the mists of time, the shifting sands of the exodus, which celebrate in imagery of thunder and earthquake the first awesome experience of God claiming Israel for his own. Then, some unknown author in exile in Babylon drew together the memories and records (some being stories to account for an age-old ruin, others being exact court records) of the centuries in Canaan. He shaped them to show that Israel's constant unfaithfulness won her the loving chastisement of God, until God could tolerate it no longer and had to suffer the shame of abandoning his people to the savagery of other peoples, serving other gods. And behind it all, right at the beginning, stand those crucial first chapters of Genesis, which almost predict what is going to happen. They analyse in story form the relationship of the world to its Creator, the grandeur and the weakness of the human creature, the ineradicable human tendency to failure when left unaided.

All these different kinds of writing were needed to express God's word, assailing first one ear, then another, in the different circumstances of each. In any case, the Bible is never dull... well, hardly ever. You may even find the prescriptions in Leviticus for the treatment of leprosy fascinating, but —unless you operate with a large-scale map of the Near East—the genealogies of Chronicles will surely provoke a yawn!

Henry Wansbrough OSB leads a course for MA in Theology at Ample-forth Abbey in Yorkshire. He is a Series Editor for The People's Bible Commentary *and the author of* Luke *in that series.*

The Editor recommends

Naomi Starkey

As Christians we believe that the Bible presents the story of God's dealings with his creation and with us, his creatures. Beginning with—literally— the very beginning, scripture takes us from the first act of rebellion in Eden and on through the unfolding of God's great rescue plan, culminating in the coming of Jesus, Messiah, Saviour of the world (and, as we know, it does not end there). We return to it again and again, studying, pondering, seeking prayerfully to discover fresh insights from its pages.

Jesus' life, death and resurrection are, of course, the supreme focus of the four Gospels, and it is there that we can turn to seek answers to the question, 'Just what exactly is so special about Jesus and what he accomplished during his life and ministry?' Even if we have not asked ourselves this question with any urgency, we will encounter it as we share our faith with others.

Focusing on just one of the Gospels is a good way of 'soaking' ourselves in who Jesus is and the significance of what he has done. *Meeting the Saviour* takes as its focus the Gospel of John, and demonstrates how its particular emphasis is on exploring the glory of Jesus, as revealed in his life, his teaching, his death and his impact on human history.

Author Derek Tidball shows how 'glory' is one of the themes of this Gospel, alongside 'light', 'life' and 'truth'. In a series of straightforward and accessible Bible-based reflections, he takes key stories and teaching in the Gospel account, showing how they portray Jesus' time on earth as, in effect, one long transfiguration. This revealed, to those able and willing to see it, the glory that is the signature of God in creation.

The book works chapter by chapter through the many different episodes and impressions of Jesus that appear in John's Gospel, considering how the apostle shaped the narrative to elucidate this theme of glory. We see Jesus as sacrificial lamb, wise teacher, eternal word, sabbath breaker, good shepherd, true vine, dying king and hope restorer, among a host of other examples. As we ponder these passages, we too can meet the Saviour, allowing ourselves to be transformed by his touch.

Derek Tidball is Principal of the

London School of Theology and was previously Head of the Mission Department at the Baptist Union of Great Britain. He has written and contributed to many books, including most recently *The Message of Leviticus* (IVP, 2005), *Wisdom from Heaven* (Christian Focus, 2003), and *The Message of the Cross* (IVP, 2001).

The transformation we experience when we encounter the risen Jesus needs to flow out into our worship and witness. As the Church, particularly in the West, struggles against decades of decline, the call has gone out to develop 'emerging churches' and 'mission-shaped' initiatives. Instead of simply attending the same old services in the same old way, Christians must work to ensure that their witness remains both prophetic and challenging—but also relevant to a rapidly changing culture. Somehow we must find ways of relating to today's world without watering down the gospel message.

Ray S. Anderson is senior professor of theology and ministry at Fuller Theological Seminary, California, known worldwide for cutting edge theological and mission thinking. In *An Emergent Theology for Emerging Churches*, he explores the parallels between the situation facing the church today and the first-century Antioch church, where the apostle Paul shaped what could be described as 'emergent theology', developing from the 'parent' Jerusalem church.

It is inspiring reading for church leaders involved in any kind of 'mission-shaped' initiative—and all those concerned about how we bear witness to the gospel today. Yes, we need to shape what we say so that our intended audience can hear our message. At the same time, though, we can heed the author's assurance that this is not about a new theology but about re-envisioning 'a vintage theology—the same, yesterday, today and forever. It is about a theology that sings as well as stings, igniting the mind and stirring the heart'.

His argument centres on the fact that what is important is building Christ-centred communities, which bear witness by what they do as much as what they say, and where the focus is on the Holy Spirit rather than just 'spirituality'. At the same time, the emphasis needs to be on mission as well as ministry, and about looking to what lies ahead and not simply pondering on what has passed into history.

A book that provides much food for thought as well as stimulus for action, *An Emergent Theology for Emerging Churches* has been warmly endorsed by a number of leading figures including Eddie Gibbs, Professor of Church Growth at Fuller Theological Seminary, Brian McLaren, and Todd Hunter, National Director of Alpha USA.

To order a copy of Meeting the Saviour *or* An Emergent Theology for Emerging Churches, *please turn to the order form on page 159.*

An extract from *Beginnings and Endings*

Advent is all about beginnings—the beginning of the Church year, of creation, of Christianity, and of the new heavens and the new earth—most of which are born out of an ending, an old era giving way to a new one. Our everyday lives are full of small-scale beginnings and endings—births, deaths, marriages. In BRF's 2007 Advent book, author Maggi Dawn reflects on six groups of people in the Bible; each provides a focus for the idea of beginnings and endings, and draws ancient wisdom from the human experience that happened in between. The following extracts are from Section 1: 'The Gospels and the salvation story'.

Early or late?

Read Psalm 27.

If you're reading this on the first of December, you may well already have had a Christmas card or two fall through your letter box. I love receiving Christmas cards, from the first ones that arrive on the first of December, to the ones that arrive with a slightly panicked message of lateness on Christmas Eve, to those that come with a sheepish apology around the third of January. Whenever they arrive, early or late, I'm always cheered up by this annual reminder of how many good friends I have.

I have to admit, though, that I find it slightly depressing that Christmas always seems to begin way ahead of schedule, when shop displays and Christmas lights go up in November or even earlier. So when the very first cards arrive on the first few days of December, I'm usually still feeling a bit 'bah-humbuggy' about it all! But by the time the last posting day is upon us and I realise I'm behind schedule, then I envy the foresight of my early-bird friends and vow to be more like them next year! Certainly Christmas can sometimes feel less like a feast to be celebrated and more like a deadline to be reached. It's often, though not always, the woman in a household who carries the stress of everything being ready for Christmas, but Christmas creates deadlines for all sorts of other people too—church leaders, school teachers, retailers, and many others. Such moments focus very sharply your sense of time, and being bound by time.

In devotional terms, though,

following the seasons of the Church year can leave us with this feeling that things never happen at the right time. The realities of life rarely match up with the mood of the Church year—they always come too early or too late. If, as we travel through Lent or Advent, life is delivering abundant joys and happiness, the sombre tone of the season never quite hits home. But it's even harder to deal with if you are feeling down or low when Christmas or Easter arrives. A few years ago a friend and I wrote to each other all the way through Lent, sharing our reflections on the season. She was a great devotee of retreats and silent space; I was the mother of a newborn baby and silent spaces were few and far between. Our Lenten experience was quite profound that year, as we were both going through extreme lows for quite different reasons. On Easter Day my friend emailed to say, 'I'm so fed up with the Church year. Resurrection? I don't think so. I feel like I need to stay in Good Friday for a good long time yet.'

All too often we have this dislocated feeling of being out of time, out of step. And Christmas is a particularly difficult season to negotiate if you don't feel like celebrating. It's not only the Church, but the whole culture that feeds us an exaggerated image of happiness

God's gifts do not always come according to our timetable

and celebration, which sets us up to feel very low if we are not in a party mood. Most of our life, though, is lived in this in-between place where things come early or late, but never on time.

Psalm 27 is sometimes given the title 'A Triumphant Song of Confidence'. I think it reads more like a defiant song than a triumphant one. The way the psalmist mixes up his tenses creates this interesting effect of reflecting on past promises fulfilled, asking for something to happen right now, stating that it's already happened, and confidently predicting that it will happen in the future. He seems at one and the same time to be giving thanks for something that is already here, and asking for help in the midst of trouble. There's an urgent anxiety about his cry for help: 'Do not cast me off, do not forsake me.' And perhaps there's even a touch of the childish promise to be good if God will only help him: 'Teach me your way O Lord, lead me on a level path.'

The psalmist's experience reminds me of the dislocation of our lives from the Church seasons. God's gifts do not always come according to our timetable, or at the moment when we think we need them. Advent and Christmas seem to promise us the presence of God, and yet it seems that sometimes God hides his face and is nowhere to be found. But God's timetable is not the same as ours, and our sense of need or urgency doesn't twist God's arm into a response.

When I was a child, we had a maiden aunt, a remarkable and wonderful woman who always, absolutely dependably, forgot all our birthdays. But at some random time of year—May or July or November—a big parcel would arrive full of presents. They might say 'Happy Birthday' or 'Happy Christmas', regardless of the time of year. It seemed madly exciting to us to get a completely unexpected present just when life was going through a tedious moment. It was always books—she taught English literature, and was bang up to date on the latest releases—and they were always wonderful. The same aunt, when we went to stay, would sneak into our bedroom just before sunrise, pull jumpers over our pyjamas, and our bare feet into shoes with no socks (against mum's rules!), and quietly lead us out of the house, leaving everyone else asleep. Then she would pile my sister and me into her very old Austin and drive us down to the beach. This was in Somerset, where the beach goes out for about two miles at low tide. There she would actually drive across the sand—again, strictly against the rules, but there's no one there at sunrise to make you obey the rules—and out of the car would

appear a primus stove, an omelette pan, eggs, butter, salt, pepper, fresh bread… We ate omelettes and drank tea as the sun rose over the sea, and then went paddling in our pyjamas, breathing in great gulps of early morning salty air. The woman was a genius, and we adored her.

Whenever I forget a Christmas card, a birthday card or whatever, I think of Aunty Margaret. Please, God, let me be like her. I hope I never become the kind of person that demands diamonds and perfume on the right date. I hope I do become the kind of person who remembers to send gifts that someone will love, instead of gifts to satisfy a deadline. And whenever God's gifts elude me, when there is no joy at Easter, no wonder at Christmas, or simply no sense of God's presence in between times, again I think of Aunty Margaret. The gift will arrive at the right moment, even if not on the 'right' date. Joy on demand is joyless indeed, but omelettes on the beach and presents in July I can seriously live with.

If we confidently depend on the knowledge that God's gifts, unlike Santa's, are not delivered to a dead-line, then we can live within the seasons knowing that the gift they represent will come to us, unex-pectedly, not necessarily on time. We can say with hope, or even a lit-tle holy defiance, 'I believe that I shall see the goodness of the Lord in the land of the living.'

Luke: Let me tell you a story

Read Luke 1:1–7.

Luke's is the only one of the four Gospels to have this kind of Prologue, a little introductory statement as to why and how the Gospel was written. It's a matter of long debate whether Theophilus was the name of a real person, or whether the name, which means 'lover of God', was Luke's way of addressing his readers personally. Either way, the opening sentence has the effect of giving some sense of relationship between the storyteller and the reader. You get the sense that Luke is writing to you personally, not just addressing some nameless, faceless crowd.

Writing to real readers is one thing that makes Luke one of the best storytellers in the Bible. Another is the fact that he makes the people inside the story seem real too. Luke gives us more than historical plot, more than philosophy and doctrine: he gives us flesh-and-blood characters that we can identify with. In particular, he is the only one of the Gospel writers who brings Jesus' family to life. Matthew tells us about the surrounding circumstances of the birth stories, but only Luke has the 'inside' information. He said in his prologue that he had carefully investigated everything 'from the start'—the start of Jesus life, perhaps? It's possible that Luke may have known members of the Holy Family, and perhaps he even knew Mary, the mother of Jesus, in person. But he certainly had a source close to the family to get hold of these personal anecdotes.

Luke is a storyteller, but one with a respect for historical sense: he says he wants it to be an 'orderly' account. And his reason for telling the story is that he wants to pass on the faith. The words he uses in the Prologue are the words of a teacher: he speaks of what has been 'handed down', taught from one group to the next, and he speaks of the story as both 'truth' and 'instruction'. Luke, then, wants to give a rational and sensible account of the events that the Christian faith is based on, and he wants to tell them in such a way that it demands personal engagement with Jesus, not just rational assent to a belief system or obedience to religious ritual.

Luke's Gospel, more than any other, tells the story of Jesus in the most humanly engaged way. Luke's characters climb off the pages and touch our heartstrings, not just our intellect. It's Luke who gave us the great emotive and personal stories of the Gospels— the parental agony and sibling rivalry of the prodigal son, the unexpected friendship of Jesus towards Zacchaeus, the weaving together of twelve years in the life of a woman and a girl, both of whom need new life, the confusion and pain of the disciples on the road to Emmaus. Luke declares his intent in the opening verses of his Gospel to give an account in the right order. The account he gives places things in time, and focuses the story on the impact of Jesus upon real people.

Luke's starting place is a focus on human interest, not on history or prophecy, but he deftly gives the story context and definition by highlighting the fact that it takes place in the context of history, politics and religion. 'In the days of King Herod of Judea, there was a priest,' he begins, and immediately tells us that the story starts in the temple in Jerusalem, the heart of first-century Judaism. It's a story about religious things but, as we shall see, a story that turns religious matters on their head. It's also a story that takes place in a political setting, in a nation under occupation, under the reign of a puppet king. That's important because the Gospel, as Luke tells it, has political consequences as well as religious ones. And he makes the story intensely personal by telling us that the priest and his wife 'were living righteously… but they had no children'. In Zechariah and Elizabeth's cultural context, to be childless was not only a personal grief but also an implied slight on their character, as childlessness carried a sense of divine judgement with it.

Luke begins, then, by telling us

> *Luke's starting place is a focus on human interest*

that the good news of Jesus happens at a moment in history to real people. He sets the scene for what will be disrupted and challenged and brought to account by the gospel, and for what will be rescued and salvaged and healed. He sets the good news of Jesus not merely in a religious setting but in the wider scheme of things. It's 'in the days of King Herod of Judea'—right in the midst of everyday life and political history, and Luke doesn't shy away from the fact that the gospel arrives in the midst of political injustice, in war zones and occupied territories, disrupting existing political and religious hierarchies. The good news is full of life and goodness, but it isn't well-behaved or polite. He also tells us that the good news is genuinely good news for real people—people who are faithful and good, but also people who are broken-hearted, for those whose hopes have been dashed, who live under a shadow because society unjustly hangs a question mark over their heads. Luke begins the good news, then, right in the heart of life: it will affect everything, political, religious, community and family. The gospel, for Luke, is not primarily conceptual. It's right here, right now, and it's thoroughly personal.

To order a copy of this book, please turn to the order form on page 159.

When You Walk

September 2007 sees the publication of a revised and expanded edition of *When You Walk*, a best-selling collection of *New Daylight* readings by Adrian Plass. Now with 365 readings, this book challenges us to explore the Bible honestly, expecting it to transform our relationship with God. Here is Adrian's introduction to twelve readings on art in the Bible, including dance, drama and architecture.

Landscapes of beauty

When this section came to mind, I felt quite excited. Some topics are so bursting with potential that it feels necessary only to plunge one's hands into the great treasure chest of scripture, scoop out armfuls of material, and then do just a little judicious editing. Occasionally it does happen a bit like that, but this time, for a long time, it did not. I simply was not able to think of a way into the theme, until, as is so often the case, I stopped thinking and did the most obvious and simple thing. I made a list. I listed all the different art forms that entered my head, from dance to dressmaking. Then I ran down the list once more, noting next to each item a place in the Bible where that particular skill or art is featured. I confess to drawing a blank on one or two, but I was amazed to discover the extent to which the arts are explicitly or implicitly mentioned in the Old and New Testaments.

I found this very invigorating. As we all know, there is a long and rich tradition of art and drama in the life of Christian communities. However, sections of the modern Church have passed through a phase of extreme wariness, especially towards artists who are unable to squeeze their productivity into the tight confines of a fear-shrunken religion. As a result, we have had to endure some Christian art that is reminiscent of those dreadful pictures from Communist Russia in which tractors seem to take centre stage. Thank God for those who have continued to follow their star as the wise men did, in order to arrive at the place where they were supposed to be, however odd the direction may have seemed. My prayer is that Christian artists will increase in numbers and confidence and be encouraged by the Bible. It rings with echoes of the wonderfully original work done by the greatest artist of all.

To order a copy of this book, please turn to the order form on page 159.

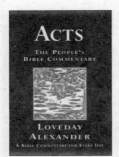

The PBC:
a map for every journey

Naomi Starkey

While the publication date of *Acts*, the final volume in BRF's *People's Bible Commentary* series, is starting to recede into memory, the BRF team is still feeling delighted at completing this mammoth project. Stretching over more than a decade from first discussions to finish, the series provides accessible commentary on every book of the Bible, using a writing team from around the world and across the denominations.

So where does the PBC sit in relation to other commentary series? It's not exactly 'entry level', but it makes no claim to be the last scholarly word in detailed textual analysis. You don't need to understand Greek or Hebrew to use the PBC; neither does the series make Bible study a brain-numbingly dry exercise. These are devotional commentaries, which aim to provide food for thought, something to take away into the day, as well as gently building up your knowledge about the passage you have read.

But why use a commentary at all? Suppose you're on a tour of the country—by car or bike, or on foot. As you survey the landscape ahead of you, what do you see? Perhaps your route is a well-trodden path, full of picturesque views and well-known landmarks. Or you might have deliberately chosen unknown territory, hoping to discover hidden

beauty along the way. Maybe you're staring out over a stretch of ground that looks, to be honest, flat and uninspiring—or a range of hills that appears too daunting for your limited horsepower, tired muscles or inappropriate footwear.

Whatever your journey promises, a good map—or a set of them—is what you need to make the most of its challenges and delights. PBCs do that job for you as you explore the various books of the Bible. They help you cross the fast rivers, plunging valleys and rocky slopes of scripture, as well as the level paths through flowery meadows.

So what is the best way to use them? If we have enjoyed using one, how do we know which one to read next? Do we have to work our way consecutively through the Bible or is there a different approach?

In response to such questions, we have come up with four reading plans, using different selections of PBC volumes, to help you navigate your way across the Bible and get a sense of how it all fits together. Each plan is for a different kind of journey, each enabling you to make sense of varied terrain.

First of all, there is the 'Way in to the Bible' plan, an accessible approach that is ideal for those who previously may not have done more than dipped into the Bible. Beginning with Mark, the shortest Gospel, it covers some of the more familiar books of Old and New Testaments (Psalms 1—72, Genesis, Ephesians to Colossians, 1 and 2 Samuel, Psalms 73—150, Hosea to Micah) and ends with Romans, Paul's great letter clarifying the foundations of Christian belief.

Alternatively, we have the 'God's working in history' plan. This reading order gives a strong sense of God at work in individual lives, amid the clash of great and ancient empires. Starting with Luke, the fullest Gospel, it passes through Ruth, Esther, Acts, Chronicles to Nehemiah, 1 Corinthians, Jeremiah and 2 Corinthians. It concludes with Deuteronomy's powerful retelling of God's choosing of Israel as his people.

Our third plan, 'Roots of our faith', is based on the fact that the roots of the Christian faith are Jewish. The reading order traces that background, starting with Matthew's Gospel and continuing with the epic Exodus narrative. It then covers Galatians and 1 and 2 Thessalonians, 1 and 2 Kings, Isaiah and Timothy to Hebrews, followed by Nahum to Malachi. In a challenging conclusion, it covers Leviticus and Numbers, two books that can appear impenetrable but richly repay close and patient study.

The final plan is called 'God's mysterious wisdom'. It starts with John, the most enigmatic of the Gospels, and covers parts of scripture, ranging from the thought-provoking to the prophetic and visionary, that can be downright unsettling! Moving on from John, the plan covers Job, Joshua and Judges, James to Jude, Daniel, Proverbs, Ezekiel and finally the book of Revelation. While some of these texts may be hard going, they can all be understood (with the help of a good commentary) as pointing to the God who chooses to reveal himself to his creatures, while ultimately remaining beyond our understanding.

Four maps; four approaches: take your pick and choose your starting point. Exploring the Bible is a crucial part of the discipleship journey, and embarking on this adventure with the help of the PBC means that there is less chance of getting lost along the way!

Single PBC volumes are priced £7.99 or £8.99. Please turn to the order form on page 159 to buy the whole collection for only £175 (saving £92), all New Testament titles for £70 (save almost £40) or all Old Testament volumes for £105 (save over £50).

Barnabas RE Days

Lucy Moore

Being 'equipped for all terrain', for the *Barnabas* team, usually means either making sure the tread on the car tyres is up to scratch for a trek to a school in the far depths of Somerset, or checking that we've included the crucial hats, treasure chests, sheep and flippers (don't ask) needed for the various stories of the day. However, I guess it could also mean equipping children for some of the different situations they meet in life, through exciting exploration of the Bible during a *Barnabas* RE Day.

As you'll know, we're very proud of our unique work in schools, bringing the Bible to life through the creative arts, and these *Barnabas* RE Days keep going down well with children and teachers alike. We get some very encouraging comments from schools:

We all very much enjoyed our day with Martyn. We found him inspiring. I loved the creation story he told my Reception class. It gave me many ideas for follow-up work. Martyn's assembly was thought-provoking and involved the whole school. We feel very privileged to have shared a day with him.

PAIVI PAYNE, CHRIST CHURCH CE PRIMARY SCHOOL, GREENWICH

It was great to have Lucy with us for the day. She brought the Bible to life in assembly and in the workshops. The children loved her enthusiasm,

fun and good ideas. We all had a different super day.

CHERYL SUTCLIFFE, MARSTON THOROLD'S CHARITY CE SCHOOL, GRANTHAM

John was very amenable and good with all the children. All staff felt the day was valuable and that the children got a lot from it. We all had a great day, thanks to all.

VAL RENOWDEN, LITTLE BLOXWICH CE VC PRIMARY SCHOOL, WALSALL

In 2006, after much team discussion, bringing together our joint experience of what works well in schools and of appropriate approaches to the Bible when working with children, we introduced a new theme to our range for *Barnabas* RE Days and started offering 'What's so special about the Bible?' to schools. Some teachers feel ill-equipped to tackle the huge questions about the Bible that are posed both by RE schemes of work and by the children themselves, so it seemed that this is another area where *Barnabas* can bring expertise to add value to the RE in a school.

I had my first attempt at the new material in a Catholic girls' school in Reading. We had a fascinating time and the girls threw themselves with great enthusiasm into various exploratory activities to do with images of the Bible, brought the story of Philip and the Ethiopian to life most dramatically and particularly relished the chance to see the bigger picture of the Bible rolled out before them. Martyn spent a day with a school in Towcester on the same theme. His report gives you a good idea of the range of activities covered, and the welcome questioning attitude of the children.

After lunch the topic changed. The sessions with Years 5 and 6 focused on the Bible itself and why it is such a special book. Once again some simple activities and drama games introduced the range and scope of the books in the Bible, the different writers and how the Bible describes itself. For the latter, the children threw themselves into creating statues that represented similes such as light, a sword, honey and a treasure chest. There were some imaginative ideas ranging from beehives to long-life

> **You can buy Barnabas gift vouchers for a school**

bulbs. Time and space (we were in the music room) meant we never got to explore any particular episode in depth but we did end each session with another reflective story, which we have called 'the story of the Story'. This tries to present how the Bible came together as the book that we know today, from the oral tradition around a campfire, via the Ten Commandments, the Torah, various scrolls of the prophets, parchments and manuscripts to the printed book. This prompted much discussion, including requests that I try to translate the Latin on the illuminated manuscript and interpret the marks on the clay tablets!

Barnabas RE Days are reaching children across the UK with insights about and from the Bible in a huge way. Perhaps this exciting ministry is something you could help to bring to a school near you? The *Barnabas* voucher scheme enables you to do just that. You can buy *Barnabas* gift vouchers for a school that can be used either towards our resources or towards the cost of a *Barnabas* RE Day. For full details, ring the *Barnabas* administrator on 01865 319704 or see our website: www.barnabasinchurches.org.uk.

Lucy Moore is an author, actor and storyteller, using her gifts as a member of the Barnabas Ministry *team.*

New Daylight © BRF 2007

The Bible Reading Fellowship
First Floor, Elsfield Hall, 15–17 Elsfield Way, Oxford OX2 8FG
Tel: 01865 319700; Fax: 01865 319701
E-mail: enquiries@brf.org.uk; Website: www.brf.org.uk

ISBN 978 1 84101 381 7

Distributed in Australia by:
Willow Connection, PO Box 288, Brookvale, NSW 2100.
Tel: 02 9948 3957; Fax: 02 9948 8153;
E-mail: info@willowconnection.com.au
Available also from all good Christian bookshops in Australia.
For individual and group subscriptions in Australia:
Mrs Rosemary Morrall, PO Box W35, Wanniassa, ACT 2903.

Distributed in New Zealand by:
Scripture Union Wholesale, PO Box 760, Wellington
Tel: 04 385 0421; Fax: 04 384 3990; E-mail: suwholesale@clear.net.nz

Distributed in Canada by:
The Anglican Book Centre, 80 Hayden Street, Toronto, Ontario, M4Y 3G2
Tel: 001 416 924-1332; Fax: 001 416 924-2760;
E-mail: abc@anglicanbookcentre.com; Website: www.anglicanbookcentre.com

Publications distributed to more than 60 countries

Acknowledgments
The New Revised Standard Version of the Bible, Anglicized Edition, copyright © 1989, 1995 by the Division of Christian Education of the National Council of the Churches of Christ in the USA. Used by permission. All rights reserved.

The Holy Bible, Today's New International Version, copyright © 2004 by International Bible Society. Used by permission of Hodder & Stoughton Publishers, a division of Hodder Headline Ltd. All rights reserved. 'TNIV' is a registered trademark of International Bible Society.

Extracts from the Authorized Version of the Bible (The King James Bible), the rights in which are vested in the Crown, are reproduced by permission of the Crown's Patentee, Cambridge University Press.

Extracts from The Book of Common Prayer of 1662, the rights of which are vested in the Crown in perpetuity within the United Kingdom, are reproduced by permission of Cambridge University Press, Her Majesty's Printers.

The Revised Common Lectionary is copyright © The Consultation on Common Texts, 1992 and is reproduced with permission. *The Christian Year: Calendar, Lectionary and Collects*, which includes the *Common Worship* lectionary (the Church of England's adaptations of the *Revised Common Lectionary*, published as the Principal Service lectionary) is copyright © The Central Board of Finance of the Church of England, 1995, 1997, and material from it is reproduced with permission.

Printed in Singapore by Craft Print International Ltd

BRF is a Christian charity committed to resourcing the spiritual journey of adults and children alike. For adults, BRF publishes Bible reading notes and books and offers an annual programme of quiet days and retreats. Under its children's imprint *Barnabas*, BRF publishes a wide range of books for those working with children under 11 in school, church and home. BRF's *Barnabas Ministry* team offers INSET sessions for primary teachers, training for children's leaders in church, quiet days, and a range of events to enable children themselves to engage with the Bible and its message.

We need your help if we are to make a real impact on the local church and community. In an increasingly secular world people need even more help with their Bible reading, their prayer and their discipleship. We can do something about this, but our resources are limited. With your help, if we all do a little, together we can make a huge difference.

How can you help?

- You could support BRF's ministry with a donation or standing order (using the response form overleaf).

- You could consider making a bequest to BRF in your will, and so give lasting support to our work. (We have a leaflet available with more information about this, which can be requested using the form over-leaf.)

- And, most important of all, you could support BRF with your prayers.

Whatever you can do or give, we thank you for your support.

BRF – resourcing your spiritual journey

BRF MINISTRY APPEAL RESPONSE FORM

Name _____

Address _____

_____ Postcode _____

Telephone _____ Email _____

(tick as appropriate)

Gift Aid Declaration

❏ I am a UK taxpayer. I want BRF to treat as Gift Aid Donations all donations I make from 6 April 2000 until I notify you otherwise.

Signature _____ Date _____

❏ I would like to support BRF's ministry with a regular donation by standing order (please complete the Banker's Order below).

Standing Order – Banker's Order

To the Manager, Name of Bank/Building Society _____

Address _____

_____ Postcode _____

Sort Code _____ Account Name _____

Account No _____

Please pay Royal Bank of Scotland plc, Drummonds, 49 Charing Cross, London SW1A 2DX (Sort Code 16-00-38), for the account of BRF A/C No. 00774151

The sum of _____ pounds on ___ /___ /___ (insert date your standing order starts) and thereafter the same amount on the same day of each month until further notice.

Signature _____ Date _____

Single donation

❏ I enclose my cheque/credit card/Switch card details for a donation of £5 £10 £25 £50 £100 £250 (other) £ _____ to support BRF's ministry

Credit/Switch card no. ❏❏❏❏❏❏❏❏❏❏❏❏❏❏❏❏❏❏❏

Expires ❏❏❏❏ Security code ❏❏❏ Issue no. of Switch card ❏❏❏❏

Signature _____ Date _____

(Where appropriate, on receipt of your donation, we will send you a Gift Aid form)

❏ Please send me information about making a bequest to BRF in my will.

Please detach and send this completed form to: Richard Fisher, BRF, First Floor, Elsfield Hall, 15–17 Elsfield Way, Oxford OX2 8FG. BRF is a Registered Charity (No.233280)

ND0307

BIBLE READING RESOURCES PACK

A pack of resources and ideas to help to promote Bible reading in your church is available from BRF. The pack, which will be of use at any time during the year, includes sample editions of the notes, magazine articles, leaflets about BRF Bible reading resources and much more. Unless you specify the month in which you would like the pack sent, we will send it immediately on receipt of your order. We greatly appreciate your donations towards the cost of producing the pack (without them we would not be able to make the pack available) and we welcome your comments about the contents of the pack and your ideas for future ones.

This coupon should be sent to:

BRF
First Floor
Elsfield Hall
15–17 Elsfield Way
Oxford
OX2 8FG

Name ——————————————————————————

Address ————————————————————————

————————————————————————————————

———————————————————— Postcode ——————————

Telephone ————————————————————

Email ——————————————————————————————

Please send me ———— Bible Reading Resources Pack(s)

Please send the pack now/ in ———————————— (month).

I enclose a donation for £ ———— towards the cost of the pack.

❏ Please send me a Bible reading resources pack to encourage Bible reading in my church

❏ I would like to take out a subscription myself (complete your name and address details only once)

❏ I would like to give a gift subscription (please complete both name and address sections below)

Your name _____

Your address _____

_____ Postcode _____

Gift subscription name _____

Gift subscription address _____

_____ Postcode _____

Please send *New Daylight* beginning with the January / May / September 2008 issue: (delete as applicable)

(please tick box)	UK	SURFACE	AIR MAIL
NEW DAYLIGHT	❏ £12.75	❏ £14.10	❏ £16.35
NEW DAYLIGHT 3-year sub	❏ £30.00		
NEW DAYLIGHT DELUXE	❏ £17.10	❏ £20.70	❏ £25.20

I would like to take out an annual subscription to *Quiet Spaces* beginning with the next available issue:

(please tick box)	UK	SURFACE	AIR MAIL
QUIET SPACES	❏ £16.95	❏ £18.45	❏ £20.85

Please complete the payment details below and send your coupon, with appropriate payment, to: **BRF, First Floor, Elsfield Hall, 15–17 Elsfield Way, Oxford OX2 8FG.**

Total enclosed £ _____ (cheques should be made payable to 'BRF')

Payment by cheque ❏ postal order ❏ Visa ❏ Mastercard ❏ Switch ❏

Card number: ☐☐☐☐ ☐☐☐☐ ☐☐☐☐ ☐☐☐☐

Expires: ☐☐☐☐ Security code ☐☐☐ Issue no (Switch): ☐☐☐☐

Signature (essential if paying by credit/Switch card) _____

BRF is a Registered Charity

BRF PUBLICATIONS ORDER FORM

Please ensure that you complete and send off both sides of this order form.
Please send me the following book(s):

		Quantity	Price	Total
497 5	Meeting the Saviour (D. Tidball)	_____	£6.99	_____
535 4	An Emergent Theology for Emerging Churches (R. Anderson)	_____	£8.99	_____
566 8	Beginnings and Endings (M. Dawn)	_____	£7.99	_____
214 8	The Promise of Christmas (F. Dorrell)	_____	£4.99	_____
526 2	The Barnabas Children's Bible (R. Davies)	_____	£12.99	_____
531 6	When You Walk (new edn) (A. Plass)	_____	£12.99	_____
314 5	PBC: Genesis (G. West)	_____	£8.99	_____
066 3	PBC: Exodus (H.R. Page)	_____	£8.99	_____
030 4	PBC: 1 & 2 Samuel (H. Mowvley)	_____	£7.99	_____
118 9	PBC: 1 & 2 Kings (S.B. Dawes)	_____	£7.99	_____
094 6	PBC: Job (K. Dell)	_____	£7.99	_____
031 1	PBC: Psalms 1—72 (D. Coggan)	_____	£8.99	_____
065 6	PBC: Psalms 73–150 (D. Coggan)	_____	£7.99	_____
151 6	PBC: Isaiah (J. Bailey Wells)	_____	£8.99	_____
087 8	PBC: Jeremiah (R. Mason)	_____	£7.99	_____
191 2	PBC: Matthew (J. Proctor)	_____	£8.99	_____
046 5	PBC: Mark (D. France)	_____	£8.99	_____
027 4	PBC: Luke (H. Wansbrough)	_____	£7.99	_____
029 8	PBC: John (R.A. Burridge)	_____	£8.99	_____
216 2	PBC: Acts (L. Alexander)	_____	£8.99	_____
082 3	PBC: Romans (J.D.G. Dunn)	_____	£8.99	_____
122 6	PBC: 1 Corinthians (J. Murphy O'Connor)	_____	£7.99	_____
073 1	PBC: 2 Corinthians (A. Besancon Spencer)	_____	£7.99	_____
012 0	PBC: Galatians and 1 & 2 Thessalonians (J. Fenton)	_____	£7.99	_____
363 3	PBC: Revelation (M. Maxwell)	_____	£8.99	_____
	PBC: Entire collection (32 volumes)	_____	£175.00	_____
	PBC: All New Testament volumes	_____	£70.00	_____
	PBC: All Old Testament volumes	_____	£105.00	_____

Total cost of books £ _____

Donation £ _____

Postage and packing £ _____

TOTAL £ _____

POSTAGE AND PACKING CHARGES

order value	UK	Europe	Surface	Air Mail
£7.00 & under	£1.25	£3.00	£3.50	£5.50
£7.01–£30.00	£2.25	£5.50	£6.50	£10.00
Over £30.00	free	prices on request		

See over for payment details. All prices are correct at time of going to press, are subject to the prevailing rate of VAT and may be subject to change without prior warning.

PAYMENT DETAILS

Please complete the payment details below and send with appropriate payment and completed order form to:

**BRF, First Floor, Elsfield Hall,
15–17 Elsfield Way, Oxford OX2 8FG**

Name _____

Address _____

_____

_____ Postcode _____

Telephone _____

Email _____

Total enclosed £ _____ (cheques should be made payable to 'BRF')

Payment by cheque ❏ postal order ❏ Visa ❏ Mastercard ❏ Switch ❏

Card number: ☐☐☐☐☐☐☐☐☐☐☐☐☐☐☐☐☐☐☐

Expires: ☐☐☐☐   Security code ☐☐☐   Issue no (Switch): ☐☐☐☐

Signature (essential if paying by credit/Switch card) _____

❏ Please do not send me further information about BRF publications.

ALTERNATIVE WAYS TO ORDER

Christian bookshops: All good Christian bookshops stock BRF publications. For your nearest stockist, please contact BRF.

Telephone: The BRF office is open between 09.15 and 17.30.
To place your order, phone 01865 319700; fax 01865 319701.

Website: Visit www.brf.org.uk

ND0307